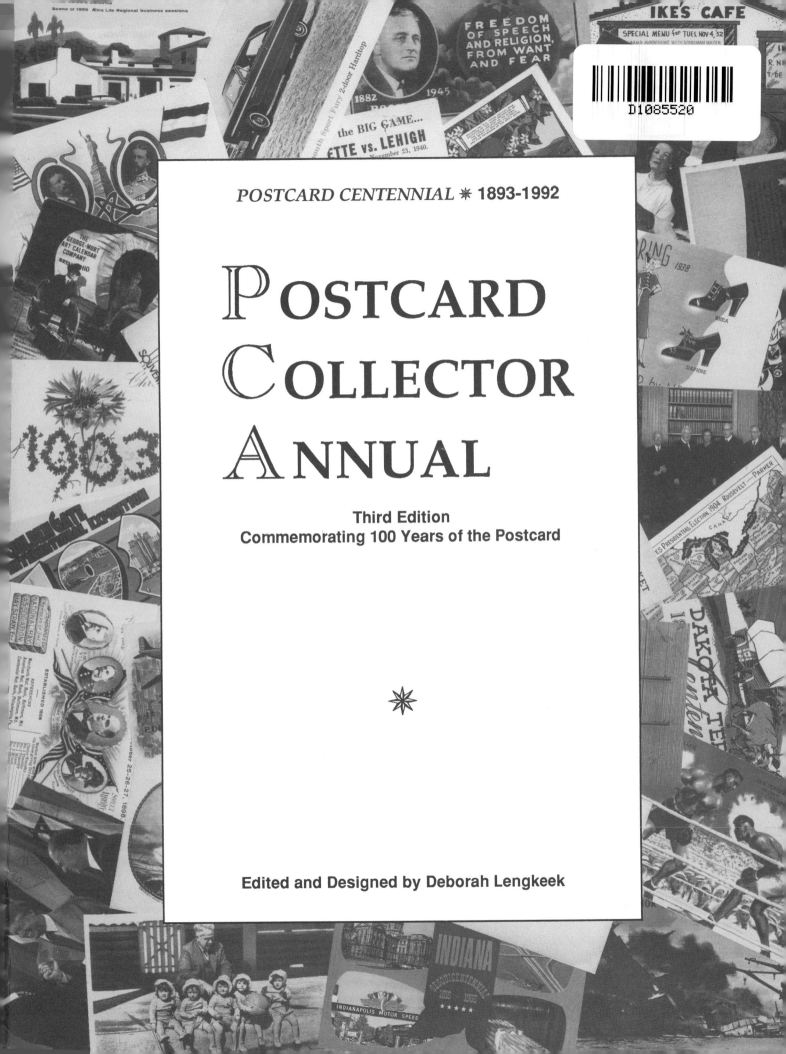

POSTCARD CENTENNIAL ✶ 1893-1992

POSTCARD

COLLECTOR

ANNUAL

Third Edition
Commemorating 100 Years of the Postcard

✶

Edited and Designed by Deborah Lengkeek

FORWARD

Even though none of us working on or reading this book were even born when postcards began weaving the rich tapestry for what is now known as the hobby of deltiology, we all benefit from the foresight of our ancestors who saved them. Much of what has gone before us has been captured on postcards—social and political history; events and products that have shaped our lives, both good and bad; where we've lived, where we've visited, or where we've never been except in our dreams.

It was hard to conceive at the beginning of this project how the last century would be brought to life within these pages. In particular, the past four decades were of great interest to me personally, as those are the times within which I have lived. It was easy to catch myself saying, "My gosh! I'd forgotten about that."

Special thanks to all of the writers who participated in the creation of this centennial celebration issue. By sharing your knowledge of the times and the many rare postcard examples, the *Postcard Collector Annual* reconstructs, decade by decade, a century of progress within the hobby.

About the cover: As a tribute to the 100th anniversary of the postcard, artist S.E. Kemp depicts the various modes of transportation used throughout the century for delivering the mail.

✳

Deborah Lengkeek

ISBN 1-879825-06-6

TABLE OF CONTENTS

ORIGIN & EVOLUTION OF THE PICTURE POSTCARD

By Bruce Nelson

Although the first postcard, now known as the Lipman card, was introduced in 1861, mass production did not begin until 1893 at the World's Columbian Exposition in Chicago. The Fisheries Building and a portrait of Christopher Columbus grace this official souvenir card, printed on a one-cent government postal and distributed by Goldsmith.

The mass introduction of the picture postcard at the World's Columbian Exposition in Chicago in 1893 met with enthusiastic public response. Originally sold in sets of four, expanded to sets of ten, then 12, high quality, multicolored lithographic images were delivered by the distributor, Goldsmith. These cards were printed on large size, one-cent government postals and contained views relating to the Exposition. Goldsmith's cards were extremely popular, as they could be mailed from the Exposition Station to anywhere in America or Canada for a penny or, if cut down to UPU standards, to Europe for an additional one-cent stamp.

Fred Megson, a specialist of Columbian Exposition postal history claims there are approximately 120 different picture cards relating to this event. The non-government postcards are exceedingly rare as they required a two-cent stamp if they had any written message. They were printed in very small quantities because there was little demand for these higher priced cards. In any case, hundreds of thousands of Goldsmith cards were bought, and untold numbers were mailed. This represented the first visible evidence that the American public was developing an interest and desire for picture postcards.

For the sake of accuracy, however, it should be pointed out that the world's first postcard was introduced and a copyright obtained by Charlton in 1861 in Philadelphia, for what became known as the Lipman card. Five copies are known to exist (Burdick); none used. In about 1871-72, the second edition Lipman card, showing the Esterbrook pen, was sent through the mail. This probably represents the first fully illustrated card in America. A few other advertising cards are known (1872-1873), and each is exceptionally rare.

Finally, in May of 1873, the United States government became the fifteenth country to introduce the penny

The original Lipman card, the world's first postcard. "Copy-Right Secured 1861."

postcard with an imprinted stamp at the one cent rate.

Over the next 20 years, the one-cent government postal (various editions) was virtually the only card used, with few exceptions. Almost all the printed illustrations placed on the card were for advertising purposes. Very few were purely greeting cards, and those few are truly classics. Any card that was sent through the mail that wasn't a government postal required a two-cent stamp if there was any written message. Since the envelope rate was also two cents, there was very little reason to send an open card through the mail that could be read by anyone during its transit. The few examples of privately printed cards that exist (1870-1893) are truly rare and are almost all advertising cards, thus qualifying for the one-cent circular rate. Even then, postal regulations were contradictory. Rules were confusing, so very few companies would risk the expense of buying a card, having it printed, and then if failing to pay the correct rate have the card end up in the dead letter office.

Front and back of the second edition Lipman card, 1871-1872. Probably the earliest known, fully illustrated American postcard, it was used to promote Esterbrook Pens.

Two other early ad cards. An illustration of the Herrick Building in New York City accompanied their notice of the company's relocation to new quarters, 1872-1873. The 1873 "Ledger Job Printing Establishment" card, Philadelphia, is unique in that it used five ink colors and seven hues to advertise "Postal Cards of Every Description." It represents the earliest known printer's postcard, showing the finest quality color lithographic work available at that time.

Finally, in 1893 with the official blessing of the postal authorities and the introduction of the Exposition viewcards, the momentum was to begin. In fact, the picture postcard began a phenomenal rise in popularity as postal regulations changed to accommodate this.

In 1894, probably in response to the success in Chicago, a set of nine cards was issued for the California Midwinter Exposition in San Francisco (January-June 1894). These cards and a few other sets are quite rare as they were not produced in great quantities due to the fact that they required a two-cent stamp for mailing. Other examples of exposition cards in the pre-1898 era are in great demand and rather rare, especially if postmarked with the exposition cancel (Cotton States—1895, Atlanta, Georgia; Tennessee Centennial—1897, Nashville,

The first U.S. government postal card, issued in 1873, cost one cent, including the imprinted stamp. Written messages were allowed without additional postage.

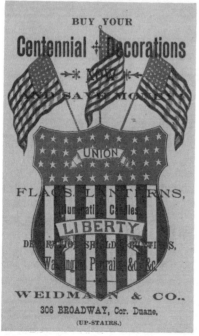

Most illustrations placed on U.S. government postals were used for advertising purposes. Shown here are several examples.

Row 1 left: 1875—Fruit jars, Abram French & Co., Boston.

Row 1 right: 1882—Stewart's Ready Roofing, New York City.

Row 2 left: 1887—"The American" pistol, Chas. B. Prouty & Co., Chicago.

Row 2 right: 1888—"Hand Fire Engine For Sale" (nearly new), H.H. Easterbrook, Boston.

Row 3 left: 1889—"Artistic Decorating" (probably the artist's own card), C.H. Koster, New York City.

Row 4 left: 1889—"Centennial Decorations" (multicolored patriotic theme), Weidmann & Co., New York City.

✳

American greeting cards on government postals are true classics. Row 3 right: 1873—"Merry Christmas and a Happy New Year" is the first known illustrated American greeting card. One of two known copies.

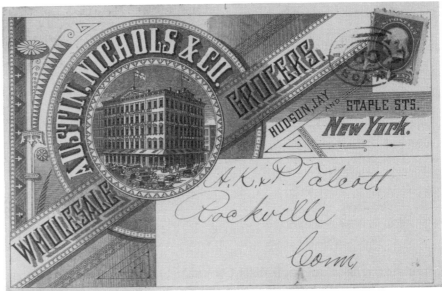

Privately printed postcards prior to 1893 are truly rare. Clockwise from top left:
*1875—"Citrate of Magnesia," Billings, Clapp & Co., Boston.
*1879—"Woodruffs Baking Powder" (multicolored), mailed in Texas.
*Circa 1880-1881—J.H. Warner, Lithographer and Printer, New York City.
*1881—A finely detailed lithography shows the office building of Austin, Nichols & Co., Wholesale Grocers, New York City.
*1883—"Hub Royal Art Stove," Smith & Anthony Stove Co., Boston.
*1887—D. Landreth & Sons Seed Farm, Philadelphia.

Right: One example from a set of nine postcards issued for the 1894 California Midwinter International Exposition in San Francisco. A correspondence card, it required a two-cent stamp.

Privately printed ad cards from the early part of this decade. Above left to right: Eli H. Sawyer, Practical Hatter, Worcester, MA, used 1893. Alberene Stone Co., New York City, used 1895. W.H. Stewart's Roof Cement and Roof Paint, New York City, used 1897. Right: "Sterling Stove," Sill Stove Works, Rochester, NY. Oversize postcard, © 1895, is also seen as a trade card.

jects around city views, especially New York and Washington, and the ships of the Great White Fleet. To make the postal rate clear to the sender, imprinted in the stamp box was: "Printed message: 1c. to any country. Written message 2c. U.S., Canada and Mexico. 5c. to any other country."

Viewcards were also popular in purely tourist areas. Niagara Falls and the White Mountains have cards generally printed on government postals, although some required adhesive stamps.

Tennessee; Trans-Mississippi—1898, Omaha, Nebraska).

Various very fine examples of privately printed advertising postcards can be found in the early years of this decade. They are usually found with advertising collectibles or philatelic collections as picture postcard collecting as we know it had not yet happened in America. Collecting postcards here began and peaked in the next decade (1903-1912), so these early cards are not in the later albums.

However, enterprising American publishers seeing the growth of the picture postcard explode in Europe, pushed for and obtained clarification of our postal regulations, and in 1896-1898 several companies came out with viewcards. One company, the American Souvenir Card Co., of New York, produced 15 different sets of cards, usually with 12 views each. (Alaska, Albany, Baltimore, Boston (two cards), Chicago, Milwaukee, New York City, Niagara Falls (summer and winter sets), Philadelphia, San Francisco, Staten Island, Voyage from New York to Europe, and Washington, D.C. One spectacular set of the Great White Fleet (below) is very hard to find. Other companies such as Kreh, Kropp, Livingston, Lowery, Rost, Strauss, and Wirth made attractive printed cards, but centered their sub-

As most postcard collectors are aware, the great printing presses of the day were in Europe, and although some American presses were of very high quality, an occasional American view during this pioneer era is found to have been printed in Europe of the finest quality. An example is illustrated below.

The Pioneer Era came to an end with the Postal

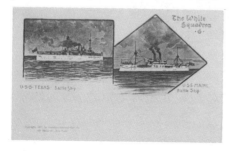

Left: The White Squadron, #6, U.S.S. *Texas* & U.S.S. *Maine*. Published by American Souvenir Card Co., NY, 1897. Right top: New York Harbor, multicolored card showing harbor and Statue of Liberty, by H.A. Rost Co., New York City, 1897. Center: Niagara Falls view on U.S. government postal, 1897. Bottom: German lithographed, multicolor Boston multiview, used 1897.

Act of May 19, 1898. Beginning July 1, 1898, postcards could be sent with or without the message for one cent. With this reduction in the postal rates and additional clarification of postal regulations, postcard publishers and printers across the country began producing the "Private Mailing Card." Even small towns had a few cards of their own. Especially popular were the multi-view cards in the European style. Tourist areas had numerous examples. Unfortunately, the printing was frequently of poor quality; the images are blurred; and although at times now quite rare, they are not especially exciting. There are, however, some excellent examples of American printing (above).

Advertising postcards of these early years are quite sought after and some are striking. In 1897, the government allowed oversized cards (8"x10"), called "The Businessman's Card." These early cards carried over into the first few years of Private Mailing Cards and were sometimes very highly illustrated. Some were sent to become store wall advertisements.

One company, Livermore & Knight of Providence, Rhode Island, produced advertising postcards of a superior quality beginning in the early 1890s, right through this ten year span. Some of their examples are among the finest known printed American cards. They specialized in multi-layered cards, shaped images, printed inserts, front and back printing, and multicolors. Most of their cards are numbered, and the ones in the 1890s are generally dated so one can obtain a real glimpse into the diversity of printing over the years. Their numbers progress to 300+ in 1902 and 1100 by 1916. These highly sought after cards are pretty much limited to New England collections as the companies they served were in that area.

Illustrated advertising on United States government postals was very common throughout this decade. Numerous examples exist, although their individual quantities were very limited due to their own market or customers. Although many are of small images and bland, the fully illustrated examples with interesting subjects are highly sought after. The cards that show guns, Uncle Sam, Santa Claus, flags, and multicolors are highly desirable.

One of my favorite groups

are the salesman announcement cards saying he will be arriving soon and "hold the orders" for him. The variety and individuality of the images are quite impressive. Frequently, the theme illustrated the method of transportation the salesman was taking to visit his customer.

Greeting cards were extremely rare during the period 1898-1901. Although beginning to be very popular in Europe, they had not yet had an impact in America. Although examples are found, their quantity is small. Also, real photo postcards were just being introduced. Scattered examples are found, usually the result of an ingenious local photographer. It was not until 1902 that the Eastman Kodak Company came out with postcard backed and sized paper upon which an image could easily be transferred. It was during the next decade however, that these became the most popular family-type card sent.

The "Private Mailing Card" era (1898-1901) was kind of a transition period in getting the American public accustomed to using postcards. If there were residual cards of earlier times, they were cut down in size and overprinted with the corrected rate. Cards of this era were required to be 3-1/4"x5-1/2" in size and on the address side printed with "Private Mailing Card—Authorized by the Act of Congress on May 19th, 1898." Only the address was allowed on this side of the card. Finally, on December 24, 1901, regulations were loosened further to allow the words "Post Card" and eliminate the requirement of printing the 1898 regulation. Even the size was allowed to deviate from the norm. This freedom was the stimulus to get the postcard industry moving into the dynamic world of communication already in evidence throughout Europe.

Several companies became productive at this time. Foremost of these was the Detroit Publishing Company, who used the photo-chrome printing process, a Swiss technique

sold to the Detroit Photographic Company in 1898. This allowed the mass production of high quality viewcards illustrating many areas of America. Other well-known publishers included the Rotograph Company and Arthur Livingston, both of New York City, the Albertype Company of Brooklyn, New York, the Mitchell Company of San Francisco, and the Hugh Chisholm Company of Portland, Maine. Also, the Tuck Company of London established an office on Fifth Avenue to distribute their cards, including their purely American lines. The year 1902 marked the end of the first decade of picture postcards and by then the people were not only using them to send messages but also had begun to select the more appropriate type card that related to the situation involved. The picture was worth a thousand words, so a real attempt to send visual quality and meaningful cards was happening. The popularity of the picture postcards was obvious. The stage was then set so the next decade (1903-1912) could become the Golden Age of postcards in America.

✱

Bruce Nelson is an avid postcard collector specializing in the early periods of their production, especially Pioneers and pre-Pioneers. Additionally, he is a dealer in all areas of antique paper and ephemera. Nelson lives with his wife and two children in Portland, Maine.

Salesman arrival notice printed on a U.S. government postal. Geo. D. Wheeler was carrying samples from the Boston firm Parker, Holmes & Co.

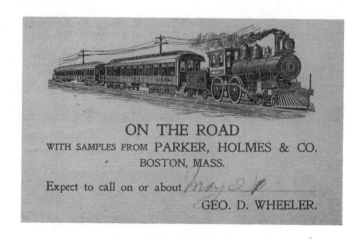

ON THE ROAD
WITH SAMPLES FROM PARKER, HOLMES & CO.
BOSTON, MASS.

Expect to call on or about _____
GEO. D. WHEELER.

AMERICA'S POSTCARD EXPLOSION

By George Miller

During this decade, all of America was dotted with shops selling postcards. Featured here is an interior view of "The House of Post Cards" in Marion, OH, published by C.G. Wiant, Bookseller & Stationer Souvenirs, and postally used in 1908.

Gather enough postcards from any ten-year period and you can re-live the decade—that's one of the great things about postcards. Through the advertisements, you can get a glimpse of technological developments and shifting consumer tastes; through views you can watch a slowly evolving landscape and an increasing urbanization; through the lowly, and often tasteless, postcard comics you can gauge the public's sense of humor and its pronounced racial and ethnic prejudices; through the "glamour" cards, you can see the vision of American youth and beauty; through its commemoratives you can document the decade's major events—social and political.

What was this decade like? In 1903, the United States had a total population of about 80 million; by 1912, the population had increased to 95 million. Throughout the decade, each year brought about one million new immigrants, almost all from Europe, so that much of the population growth came from the large numbers of Europeans flowing into the country.

The average life expectancy in 1903 was 50.5 years (compared with 75.4 today); by 1912, it had increased to 53.5 years. The average compensation for a full-time employee in 1903 was $477; by 1912, it had risen to $633. In exchange, workers put in long hours—ten-hour days, six-day weeks were common, and even skilled workers in the manufacturing industries averaged 51-hour weeks.

Certainly one of the areas in which the greatest change came was in easier access to communication and increased mobility. In 1903, the U.S. had 2.8 million telephones, an average of 34.5 telephones for every 1000 people. By 1912, the number of telephones had shot up to 90.7 million; now about one out of ten Americans had a telephone. Long distance calling, however, was financially out of the question—a three-minute call from New York City to Denver cost $11.25.

Postal services improved, especially in the rural areas. By 1906, most of the rural delivery routes had been established. At the same time, the number of post offices declined—from 74,169 in 1903 to 58,729 in 1912, marking in part a shift from rural America toward an increasingly urban America. The U.S. postal service handled 8.9 billion pieces of mail annually in 1903; that number shot up to 17.6 billion in 1912—no doubt postcards played a significant role in that increase.

Roads also improved. In 1904, the country boasted 154,000 miles of surfaced roads. By 1912, that number had risen to 231,000. The greatest jump, however, was in the number of automobile registrations. In 1903, only 32,900 automobiles were registered in this country; that number rose by almost 30 times by 1912—to 901,500. In 1903, the horse and buggy dominated American roads; by 1912, the "horseless carriage" was a common sight.

What's most distinctive about postcards during this period is their sheer number. The period between 1903 and 1912 marks the Golden

Age of postcards in the United States, the decade during which the postcard exploded into every aspect of American life. Postcards were everywhere. *American Magazine* recorded: "Bookstores which formerly did a thriving trade in literature are now devoted almost entirely to their sale. There were in Atlantic City last season ten establishments where nothing else was sold, and Chicago, Boston, Pittsburgh, and New York have emporiums where postals constitute the entire stock...These wares may be seen in New York on practically every street corner and most of the drug stores, cigar stands, hotels, barber shops and department stores."

As Bruce Nelson's article clearly demonstrates, postcards had been a part of American life—particularly as souvenirs and advertisements—for at least 30 years prior to 1903. Although a large number of different Pioneer and Private Mailing Card postcards survive, the postcard did not really "arrive" as a big business in the United States until roughly 1903-1904. You can confirm that date just by checking the cancellations on postcards sent through the U.S. mail.

That subjective assessment of the "rise" of the postcard in American society can be confirmed in a number of ways. One particularly valuable way is to document the growth of the U.S. postcard industry through the city business directory. A business directory is similar to the Yellow Pages of a telephone book; it is a list arranged alphabetically by subject of the various businesses and industries in a given area.

As a test case, a number of years ago I studied the city directories for several of the largest U.S. cities. What I was looking for was the growth of the wholesale and retail trade in postcards, judged by the number of businesses that listed themselves under the heading "Postal Cards, Illustrated." The key city in the U.S. postcard industry was New York. Foreign-based publishers and printers opened New York offices in the hopes of attracting the large east coast market. In addition, many of the early U.S. postcard printers were based in New York as well.

What I found confirmed my assumptions. If you were looking for a printer or publisher of postcards in New York prior to 1902, you would have had a difficult time. Although there were plenty of postcards printed and sold in New York prior to 1902, no business identified itself as a publisher, printer, or seller of postcards.

However, beginning in 1903 and moving through 1912, the Golden Age, watch what happened to the number of businesses (both wholesale and retail) listed under the heading "Postal Cards, Illustrated":

Number of businesses listed in the *Trow Business Directory of Greater New York*.		The same pattern was repeated in Chicago, although the "boom" came just a few years later.	
1903....... 3	1909 ... 168	1903 0	1908 8
1905 14	1911 ... 153	1904 1	1909 10
1906 48	1912 ... 124	1905 2	1911 40
1908 166		1906 3	1912 30
	✳	1907 6	1913 22

How can you focus on the development of the postcard in the era in which everything about the postcard changed and developed? I've selected ten topics/areas where I think the intersection between the development of the postcard and of American society seems particularly important. The postcard, while ephemeral, nevertheless both mirrored and shaped our society. In an age before radio and television, before extensive and sophisticated marketing strategies, before heavily illustrated magazines and newspapers, the postcard brought images and values into people's lives.

The selling and collecting of postcards: Given that this decade saw phenomenal growth in the use and sale of the postcard, topic number one has to be the selling and collecting of postcards. The bulk of postcards advertising postcards date from after 1903 but before 1912. In addition, postcard collecting clubs flourished during the period. For example, the largest American postcard club, Jolly Jokers, was formally organized in June of 1906. The club grew at a prodigious rate; less than one year after its founding, its membership was over 2300 and the Jolly Jokers' organization had spread to 25 states. That growth is a good indication of the meteoric rise of postcard collecting that occurred during this decade.

The popularization of photography and the real photo postcard: By 1902, Eastman Kodak was producing a postcard-size developing paper on which images could be printed directly from negatives. In 1903, Kodak took the real photo postcard a step further by introducing the first inexpensive camera designed to take postcard-size (3-1/4" x 5-1/2") negatives. Photography, which had originally required the skills of an amateur scientist, was now safely and easily placed into the hands of every person. The real photo postcard, which is so obsessing collectors today, was born during this decade.

American expositions, fairs, exhibits: Prior to 1903, America had seen a number of important expositions and fairs—the

Velox, a photographic developing paper, marketed, among other sizes, as a pre-imprinted postcard stock. Invitations to local demonstrations of Velox liquid developer and paper were mailed out to prospective customers. Here is an invitation to a demonstration in Hartford, CT, on March 14, 1904. Quite a few different images appear on these "Velox postal cards."

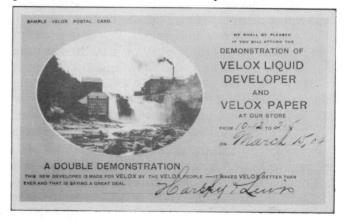

Left: An Albertype view of Italy's building at the St. Louis World's Fair. Right: An attractive poster advertisement for the Alaska-Yukon-Pacific Exposition in Seattle in 1909, published by Edward Mitchell of San Francisco.

World's Columbian in Chicago (1893), the California Midwinter (1894), the Cotton States (1895), the Trans-Mississippi (1898), the Pan-American (1901), and the South Carolina Inter-State (1901-02). None of these expositions, however, produced a really extensive range of different postcards.

With the opening of the Universal Exposition of 1904, more popularly known as the St. Louis World's Fair or the Louisiana Purchase Exposition, in April of that year, the postcard souvenir exploded in number and form. With the St. Louis Expo, collectors saw mechanical postcards, hold-to-light postcards, woven silks, wooden postcards, honeycombs, an incredible array of advertising issues given away by exhibitors, and a broad range of "official" and "unofficial" views, often coming in large sets of numbered cards. You could spend a lifetime (and a small fortune) just collecting cards from this one exposition.

The decade saw three more expositions, none of which was as large as St. Louis, but all of which produced extensive numbers of postcards: the Lewis and Clark Centennial and the American Pacific Exposition and Oriental Fair, Portland, Oregon (June-October 1905); Jamestown Tercentennial Exposition, (April-November 1907); and the Alaska-Yukon-Pacific Exposition, Seattle (June-October 1909).

In addition, postcards were issued for an astonishing array of small festivals and local celebrations. Some of the finest examples of postcard poster advertisements come from this period's festivals. Some, like the Hudson-Fulton Celebration (September 25-October 9, 1909), seemingly a small, short, and very local celebration, produced a prodigious array of different cards, far out of proportion to what one would have expected.

Political campaigns: Political campaigns were certainly not new to this decade. Again, however, what was different about this period was the magnitude of the role the postcard played. Postcards from the 1900 campaign do exist, but they are few in number and quite scarce. With the campaigns of 1904, 1908, and 1912, the postcard became an increasingly important propaganda tool. The high point in the quantity and range of different cards probably came in 1908, with literally hundreds of different designs, including a broad range of mechanicals.

In the 1904, 1908, and 1912 campaigns, voters were not limited to voting for just Republicans and Democrats; they were offered a range of alternative parties. Eugene Debs was the Socialist Party choice in all three campaigns; the Prohibition Party ran candidates in all three; Teddy Roosevelt re-emerged as a presidential candidate for the Progressive ("Bull Moose") Party in 1912.

Automobiles, airplanes, and trains: This decade saw the development and widespread popularity of the automobile. Auto companies proliferated and many used the postcard as a way of promoting their models and its virtues. In August 1903, the first transcontinental automobile journey was completed; it took a mere 52 days to drive from San Francisco to New York. In October of 1908, Henry Ford introduced the Model T at a cost of $850. Automobile ownership, as noted earlier, rose at an astonishing rate.

So widespread was the use of the postcard in the presidential campaigns of 1908 and 1912 that many issues survive that just commemorated local visits. Here, Taft in an airplane, promises to be in Hutchinson, KS.

Aviation was literally born during this decade. In December 1903, Orville Wright stayed aloft for 12 seconds, becoming the first man to fly a powered heavier-than-air machine. Aviation understandably fascinated the American public. Every large carnival and state fair was likely

A convict camp in Southern Georgia. The yellow and black stripes, double-decked movable cages and other equipment was an often encountered feature of the "Dixie Trail" laid out by the Flanders "20" Glidden Pathfinder.

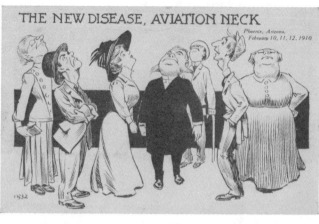

THE NEW DISEASE, AVIATION NECK

Phoenix, Arizona, February 10, 11, 12, 1910

Left: Automobile races—actually endurance contests—were popular during the decade and sets of cards were issued to commemorate some. Here one of a set of 12 cards showing the Flanders "20" on the 1911 Glidden Tour, which ran from New York City to Jacksonville, FL. Right: A stock comic imprinted here for an airshow at Phoenix, AZ, on February 10-12, 1910. The sender noted: "I am lots better and shall be fine by the time we have the meet. Come out and have a sail in my airship. Horace."

to have some display of balloons, dirigibles, and airplanes. The first U.S. air meet was held in 1910 near Los Angeles; the first American-English meet—the Harvard-Boston—was held in September 1910; the International Aviation Meet in Chicago in 1911 attracted an international field of pilots and planes. Not only did all of these events—and like others—find their way onto increasingly larger numbers of postcards, but airplanes and balloons became common greeting card motifs.

Trains had been around for a long time by 1903, but some new developments figure significantly on postcards. In October 1904, the first section of the New York subway opened; in 1905 the "Twentieth Century Limited" began 18-hour service between New York and Chicago. The era of "named" trains and rail luxury was born.

Peace, war, and international relations: The decade began with a peace conference. In May 1905, Japan asked President Teddy Roosevelt to mediate in the Russo-Japanese War, which had been raging since February 1904. The Russo-Japanese Peace Conference, held at Portsmouth, New Hampshire, August to September 1905, produced a settlement which won President Roosevelt a Nobel Peace Prize in 1906, but also resulted in increased hostility between the U.S. and Japan. The 1907 voyage of the Great White Fleet around the world, surely the most interesting naval

event of the decade, was in part an outgrowth of Roosevelt's desire to assert America's strength as a world power in the Pacific.

The Panama Canal figures prominently in events of the decade. In November 1903, the U.S. signed a treaty with Panama, leasing the Canal Zone. In November 1906, President Teddy Roosevelt visited the Panama Canal Zone, the first trip outside of the U.S. ever made by a president in office. In 1907, Roosevelt appointed Colonel George W. Goethals as chief engineer. Construction of the Canal continued throughout the decade, and not surprisingly views of the construction made their way onto many postcards.

Left: Teddy Roosevelt fascinated the American public and he, his family, and his adventures were constantly celebrated on postcards. Here the "Route Map" from a set of "Roosevelt's Tour" of Africa published by Arthur Capper in Topeka, KS. Right: A North Pole comic published by F.A. Moss in 1909. Rather than take sides—Cook or Peary—many publishers just choose to celebrate the fact that either way, the "Pole" was now "American."

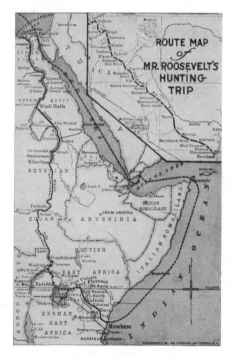

ROUTE MAP of MR. ROOSEVELT'S HUNTING TRIP

THE LIDS ON HERE TO STAY!

6438 ©FAMOSS

By the end of the decade, the U.S. was increasingly involved in Latin America. In March 1911, 20,000 U.S. troops were sent to the Mexican border. In August 1912, U.S. Marines landed in Nicaragua. Armed conflict in the area was only a year or two away.

Polar exploration: The race to the North Pole preoccupied Americans during the decade and produced a wide range of postcards celebrating the achievements of Robert E. Peary and Dr. Frederick Cook. Cook claimed to have reached the pole in April 1908; Peary in April 1909. Although Cook's claims were questioned by many, both men—and their adventures—were popular postcard subjects.

Suffrage: The decade saw a slow, but steady increase in the national campaign to secure women the right to vote. By 1912, women could vote in only 10 states and the big national demonstrations lay a year in the future. However, many of the nicest suffrage postcard sets date from this decade, including the Duston-Weiler (1909), the Wellman (1909), and the Cargill (1911). As incredible as it might now seem, the Nineteenth Amendment to the Constitution did not become law until August 1920.

San Francisco earthquake: The greatest disaster of the decade came on April 18, 1906, with the San Francisco earthquake, resulting in the death of about 700 people and damage estimated at $400 million. Since local newspapers carried no photographs, many Americans could only see the results of the devastation on postcards. For example, the Hearst newspapers carried two different series of earth-

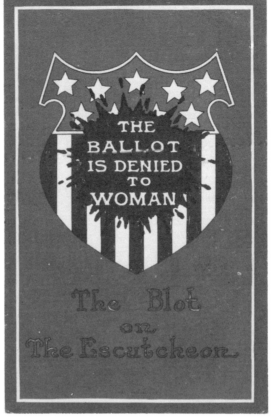

An attractive poster design from the 1910 Cargill suffrage set, "endorsed and approved by the National American Woman Suffrage Association."

quake cards offered as "supplements" to the Sunday paper which were widely distributed in 1906. Although San Francisco earthquake cards are not especially sought by collectors today, in fact several hundred different cards at least were available during the decade.

Statehood: The decade saw the admission into statehood of the final three western states. In 1907 Oklahoma became the 46th state; in 1912, New Mexico, the 47th; and Arizona, the 48th. In some symbolic way, these events marked the end of "the last frontier."

W hat is common to all of these topics is growth. American society was growing and changing, becoming less isolationistic, more urbanized, more diverse, more technologically sophisticated. The postcard was there to record it all. It seems as if nothing during the period between 1903 and 1912 escaped being recorded on a postcard. Moreover, the sheer numbers of postcards are overwhelming. Something as seemingly minor as a Russo-Japanese Peace Conference in Portsmouth, New Hampshire, in 1905 produced maybe as many as 50 different postcards; something as large as the St. Louis World's Fair probably at least several thousand different postcards.

At the time postcard publishers and retailers expected that the postcard explosion would last indefinitely. But it didn't. Even by 1912, the industry was cutting back, a change that can be seen even from the lists of postcard businesses reproduced earlier. Postcards didn't disappear, but they never again so dominated American consciousness.

✳

George Miller has been a regular contributor to *Postcard Collector* since its inception. In addition to collecting and writing about postcards, George is a professor of English at the University of Delaware.

A Franz Huld commemorative of the San Francisco earthquake in 1906.

The San Francisco Disaster
April 18th—April 23d, 1906

THE WHIRLWIND YEARS OF TUMULT

By Ruth Lechter Sabo

There was not one quiet year in this tumultuous decade that began with the riotous march for women's suffrage and ended with the Jazz Age. Here, man and his best friend remain neutral on the "Votes for Women" debate. One of ten designs from "Neutral" comic series no. 2178 by the Auburn Post Card Manufacturing Company, Auburn, IN.

It was the best of times. It was the worst of times. These famous words of Dickens aptly describe the whirlwind years of 1913-1922, a period of world war, deadly influenza, workers' strikes and revolutions, Einstein's general theory of relativity, massive immigration, prohibition, socialism, women's suffrage, the Panama Canal, the income tax, Babe Ruth, the automobile, Charlie Chaplin, Jazz, the first female member of Congress, and the first birth control clinic. Nearly all these events were captured on picture postcards, for despite 1913 being the beginning of the end of the Golden Age of the picture postcard in the United States, it is reported that nearly one billion cards were mailed that year!

In politics, the era began with the inauguration of Governor Woodrow Wilson of New Jersey as only the second Democrat elected president since before the Civil War. His inaugural parade was depicted on a wonderful black and white card by the George S. Graves Co. of Springfield, Massachusetts and Washington, D.C. Other real photo cards of the inauguration were published by I & M

300,000 enthusiastic Americans witnessed Woodrow Wilson's inaugural parade, shown here on a George S. Graves Company card.

Ottenheimer of Baltimore. The dynamism, liberal reforms, and trustbusting begun under Theodore Roosevelt continued, despite his defeat by Wilson in 1912 in a three-way race with Taft.

Workers' lives were hard in the early 20th century. Strikers often were massacred; sweatshops and child labor were prevalent; and wages were pitifully low. Wilson responded by supporting workers' compensation laws, anti-child labor statutes, and legalization of picketing. Conservative judges struck down many of

PRESIDENT WOODROW WILSON'S INAUGURAL PARADE: Pennsylvania Ave., Washington, D. C. Pennsylvania Ave., 6,000 feet long between the Capitol grounds and Treasury building and 160 feet wide, with its 300,000 ENTHUSIASTIC AMERICANS witnessing THE INAUGURAL PARADE. W-347

his reforms, but others eventually went through. In 1913 the 17th amendment authorizing direct election of U.S. senators (instead of by state legislatures) was ratified. Trustbusting continued, and Standard Oil was split up. Wilson pushed hard for the creation of the Federal Reserve Bank to help reduce the power of the money trusts on Wall Street. Tariffs were greatly reduced, and the lost revenue replaced by the nation's first graduated income tax. In 1916 child labor laws were passed.

For many, the reforms were insufficient. The anarchist Emma Goldman called for revolution, not reform. In the 1912 election that put Wilson in office, the Socialist candidate, Eugene Debs, polled nearly one million votes, and postcards depicting candidate Debs are highly prized. In fact, all campaign postcards after the 1908 race, including those from Wilson's two campaigns and Harding's 1920 campaign are difficult to find and are increasing steadily in value.

Campaign postcards did more than portray the events of the day. Their messages and images were designed to influence and shape the attitudes of the public, as did many other cards which can be considered nothing less than pieces of propaganda. One favorite is an amusing prohibition image (left) depicting a woman saying, "Lips that touch liquor shall never touch mine." Bamforth comics published farcical temperance cards, and the Women's Christian Temperance Union also published propaganda postcards. The prohibition movement had

FOR PRESIDENT

EUGENE V. DEBS

PRESIDENT WOODROW WILSON

Political opponents Eugene V. Debs and Woodrow Wilson. Left: Reproduction of Debs campaign poster by Museum Press Inc., Washington, D.C. Right: Published by B.S. Reynolds Co., Washington, D.C.

become closely affiliated with the women's suffrage movement, with many prohibition leaders also being voting rights activists. During this era, state after state passed prohibition laws, culminating in the ratification of the 18th amendment to the Constitution in January 1919, prohibiting alcoholic beverages throughout the country.

The women's suffrage movement, a favorite topic for postcard art, was relatively quiet in the first decade of the century, but gained momentum during the second. In March 1913, a huge march was organized in Washington by the National Woman Suffrage Association to coincide with Wilson's inauguration. The thousands of men and women from all over the country who gathered at the nation's Capitol were escorted by the U.S. Cavalry. Hecklers got out of control and chaos ensured. Real photo postcards of this march published by I & M Ottenheimer Co. of Baltimore are highly prized.

Also extremely popular are the delightful printed cards of this movement, featuring many of the most sought after postcard artists, such as Rose O'Neill, Ellen Clapsaddle, Walter Wellman, Cobb Shinn, and Bernhardt Wall. One comic card depicts two women strenuously arguing about "votes for women," while a man with a large "I AM NEUTRAL" sign runs away from them, ably portraying the confusion many felt about the issue. After several decades of debate and struggle, women finally won the right to vote in 1920, during Wilson's second administration. Ironically, this was four years after the first woman was elected to the House of Representatives (Jeannette Rankin from Montana).

Margaret Sanger knew that poverty and oppression would not decline until women were able to control their fertility. She made headlines throughout this period, courageously leading the birth control movement despite constant harassment and persecution. On October 16, 1916, she opened the first family planning clinic in the United States in Brooklyn, New York, (and her grandson, Alexander Sanger, now heads it). Clinics currently are located in every state in the nation, with many still under siege today, as was that first one in Brooklyn.

The world was evolving very rapidly during Wilson's presidency, and the way people transported themselves from place to place repre-

"LIPS THAT TOUCH LIQUOR SHALL NEVER TOUCH MINE"

IN AN AUTO
I remember the day we sped away
On a joy ride over the plain.
'Twas a jolly ride with you by my side,
May I have the pleasure again?

sents one of the major transformations of everyday life. In 1915, in Detroit, Michigan, an entrepreneur named Henry Ford watched his one millionth car roll off the automobile assembly line he originated two years earlier. The assembly line transformed the manufacturing world, and the automobile soon replaced streetcars, trains, bicycles, and boats as the principle modes of transportation. Postcards were there, of course, to capture this change, as well as to document its widespread use in courtship situations, as in a beautiful card by F. Earl Christy of a young couple "In An Auto." The popularity of the automobile led to a frenzy of new construction of paved roads, bridges, and tunnels, providing employment to many thousands of construction workers and engineers.

This also was the period when aviation emerged from its infancy. Airmail began in this decade. Early planes and airships were frequently depicted on picture postcards, and the entire topic of transportation cards is eagerly collected by many deltiologists.

In the United States the picture postcard era was launched with the World's Columbian Exposition in 1893, and expositions became (and remain to this day) a favorite topic of postcard art. The Panama Canal opened with much fanfare in August 1914, and it was commemorated by the Panama Pacific International Exposition in San Francisco, which was attended by an estimated 13 million people and pictured on many beautiful cards.

The early part of the century was a time of massive immigration into the United States. Most immigrants settled in large cities, especially New York City, and in enclaves of people from the same country as themselves. A particularly huge wave of Jewish immigrants came to America at this time, the majority from Russia and Eastern Europe. Some of the most interesting viewcards of this period capture the daily hustle and bustle of the life of these immigrants, such as the peddlers

and pushcarts of Hester Street, in the lower East Side of Manhattan. Other cards satirized both the physical characteristics of different immigrant groups and their occupational choices, such as the Irish cop and the Italian produce peddler.

This period of time had its superstars in the entertainment and sports worlds, as does the current decade. No less than the likes of Charlie Chaplin, Mae West, Will Rogers, Jack Dempsey, Babe Ruth, and Ty Cobb were household idols between 1913 and 1922. It also was during this period that jazz became popular; Puerto Rico was made a United States territory; and the first Jewish Justice of the Supreme Court, Louis Brandeis, was appointed. One quarter of the United States population caught the life-threatening Spanish flu, and the Bolshevik revolution in Russia influenced the entire rest of the century, but without question the central event of this era was the "war to end all wars."

On July 28, 1914, the Austrian Archduke Ferdinand was assassinated by a Serb. In no time at all Germany had joined Austria in a war against the Allied Powers of England, France, and Russia, and the First World War had begun. Wilson declared the United States neutral, but the Allies were as determined to bring America into the war on their side as the

Germans were to keep the United States out of it. The United States published a number of "neutrality" postcards, but many pro-German (where many cards were printed) and pro-Allied forces cards made their way to America's shores.

When a German submarine torpedoed the *Lusitania,* the world's largest passenger ship, on May 7, 1915, pressure to fight the Germans increased. I have a postcard (above) mailed four days after the incident addressed to a woman with a German sounding surname and with the hateful message, "You Germans must leave the country." Not everyone had such strong feelings, however,

Hester Street, New-York.

Like the immigrants on Hester Street in New York, this postcard was also imported from Europe (Germany).

When THIS GENTLEMAN, takes off his coat —he means business

I WANT YOU FOR U.S. ARMY

NEAREST RECRUITING STATION

Liberty Bonds Guarantee Humane Treatment for the Aged

make the future safe for the aged

We want no mock Prussian pensions of less than a dollar weekly for our aged. Sturdy independence of the family unit guarantees security to Democracy's mothers and fathers. Be thrifty. Save your money and invest with the Government. Save to buy.

buy liberty bonds to keep

LIBERTY LOAN COMMITTEE OF NEW ENGLAND

A massive propaganda effort was undertaken once war was official in the U.S. Here are just some of the postcard examples that were used to shape pro-Allied sentiments. Clockwise from top left: Uncle Sam rolls up his sleeves in preparation for a tough fight. Reproduction of James Montogomery Flagg's World War I poster by Dover Publications, Inc., Mineola, NY. The purchase of liberty bonds promised a victory in the war and humane treatment for the aged. U.S. Signal Corps photo of a "daring American fighter braving Hun machine gun nests..." reproduced by Photo Repro Co. "Who The 'H---' Tied This Knot?" by Albert H. Bremer, carried a hateful message on the back (see previous page). Proceeds from the sale of this cute puppy postcard went for the relief of the Allies and was produced by the Standard Art Co., NY.

DARING AMERICAN FIGHTER BRAVING HUN MACHINE GUN NESTS, SETTING OFF A SMOKE POT TO HIDE OUR INFANTRY ADVANCE.

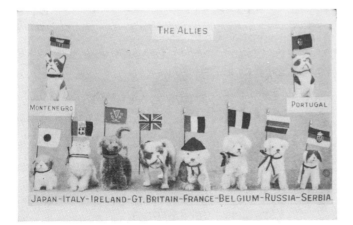

THE ALLIES

MONTENEGRO

PORTUGAL

JAPAN-ITALY-IRELAND-GT. BRITAIN-FRANCE-BELGIUM-RUSSIA-SERBIA.

Who The 'H---' Tied This Knot ?

and a large number of Americans, and especially the Socialists, believed the United States should remain neutral. Although Wilson won a second term in 1916 against Republican Charles Evans Hughes, partly on the slogan, "He kept us out of war," Wilson had been preparing for the inevitable. One month after his second inauguration, he declared war against Germany.

Once war was official, a massive propaganda effort was made to shore up anti-German sentiment. Naturally, postcards were part of that propaganda effort, helping to shape pro-Allied sentiments, with many cards printed depicting a powerful Uncle Sam taunting a cowering Kaiser Wilhelm. There is a particularly engaging series by an unknown publisher, the Comical Kaiser Series (No. 703) depicting an angry Uncle Sam easily disposing of a spineless Kaiser. What is probably the most well-known American poster of all times, a determined Uncle Sam with his arm out saying, "I want YOU for the U.S. Army," by James Montgomery Flagg, also has been depicted on postcards.

Other postcards show children seeing their fathers off to the front, and one fascinating real photo card depicts a "daring American fighter braving Hun machine gun nests, setting off a smoke pot to hide our infantry advance." The Red Cross issued a number of interesting cards, many with patriotic sentiments. There is a fascinating sepia-toned card printed by the Liberty Loan Committee of New England, under the U.S. Treasury Department, urging the recipient to invest in liberty bonds to safeguard the family unit.

The healthy and well-supplied American forces were critical to the defeat of the Germans, and finally on November 11, 1918, the Kaiser agreed to an armistice. Postcards of the troops returning home, and cards used to inform members of different troops about reunions, are scarce and valuable. From the point of view of deltiologists, the war with Germany resulted in the final nail in the coffin for the Golden Age of postcards. Not only many cards, but

Uncle Sam shows Kaiser Wilhelm "the way out" of the war. One of 12 designs from Comical Kaiser Series No. 703.

most of the best cards, had been printed in Germany. The war, combined with high tariffs, ended the importation of those cards.

President Wilson worked hard for a just and fair peace, but power rivalries in Europe resulted in the vengeful Treaty of Versailles, requiring huge reparations from Germany leading to a bitterness that helped fuel the Second World War. Wilson returned to the United States from Versailles to see his country in the turmoil typical of post-war years. Inflation was rampant, and workers went on thousands of strikes to protect the wage gains they had made. There were new waves of immigrants. Widespread fear prevailed that workers would start a revolution similar to the Bolshevik one, and this fear coupled with the similar general disruption, produced a major backlash. Wilson was debilitated by a stroke, and federal agents rounded up more than 3000 people who were denied basic due process rights, including the right to be represented by counsel. Eventually more than 500 were deported.

This period of turmoil paved the way for the Presidential election of an unknown Republican, Warren G. Harding, who campaigned on the slogan, "Back to Normalcy." Unfortunately for most citizens, his normalcy was to bust unions, ease up anti-trust enforcement, and look the other way while lynchings increased and his cronies robbed the Navy's strategic Teapot Dome oil reserves. Legislation was passed drastically cutting immigration quotas and racism surged, with the Ku Klux Klan claiming five million members at its peak.

There was not one quiet year in this tumultuous decade that began in 1913 with the riotous march for women's suffrage and ended with the Jazz Age.

✳

The Wilson era experienced too much tumult to allow another Democrat in office. Republican Warren G. Harding promised a return to normalcy. This limited edition card (1 of 2000) was published by M.A. Sheehan, Topanga, CA, from a handmade original serigraph.

Ruth Sabo has a Ph.D. in developmental psychology. She is currently a lobbyist in the state of New York and a free-lance writer for *Postcard Collector*. Ruth is married to Al Sabo, a trial lawyer who collects stamps and antique legal documents, and they have three children.

POSTCARD HOBBY REACHES ALL-TIME LOW

By George Gibbs

On rare occasions truly wonderful cards turn up showing various vehicles of the Bonus Army marchers, posed at this spot with the Capitol dome looming up behind. The message on the side of this Toledo, OH, caravan is a political parody of the 23rd Psalm, beginning, "Hoover is our Shepherd/We are in want/He maketh us lie/Down on park benches/He leadeth us beside the still factories/He disturbeth our soul..." Real photo. Value $150-$175.

For the postcard aficionado, the 1920s were a paradox. Popularly known as the "Roaring '20s"—those years of supposed economic well-being and social conviviality—shouldn't the postcard as an art form have been on the upswing? Why did those mailed mementos sink into what was their greatest decade of decline of any during this century? Between the Golden Age of postcards and those wonderful, gaudy linens, postcard creativity experienced a prolonged curve of depression upon which the Crash of '29 was merely a blip. Just thumb through a box of white border views and you will soon experience that depression first hand. Poorly lithographed, static images of roadside tourist courts, hotels, generic scenery, and lifeless main streets abound. Gone are the intimate real-photo and crisp German-made photogravure views filled with animation and sparkle of an earlier era. America grew tired of the postcard view in the 1920s, leaving its production to professionals who seemed to have the formula for covering a town down pat. Nor do the greeting cards and miscellaneous topics offer much relief. Apart from the rare Winsch orange-bordered Halloweens, flapper comics, some advertising cards with Art Deco styling, and a few special event related (such as those for Lindbergh's flight), the situation is equally bleak (left).

The reason for the decline stretches back as far as

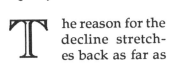

This white border view is typical of this decade's style, though the subject is not—a Panama Indian youth studying *National Geographic* magazine! Value $6-$8.

1909, when protective tariffs led to the disappearance of European imports and, as competition lessened, a decline in the quality of the American product. World War I sounded the death knell for cards lithographed in Germany. By the 1920s, folded greeting cards had become the rage. Though considerably costlier at five cents each, as opposed to postcards which sold for as little as 12 for ten cents, the quality and graphics were much superior, and a new, largely urban population could afford them.

The 1920s are commonly thought of as an age when morals loosened, hemlines rose, and the pace of life quickened. One does not need to search far for reasons: first of all, small matters of morality seemed less important in contrast with the massive carnage of the First World War. Secondly, prohibition set the tone by turning a sizeable proportion of the population into scofflaws, who would patronize speakeasies or drive just south of the border for a short one. Another reason can be found in the mass migration of Americans to the cities; in 1920 a majority of the population was urban. The Harlem Renaissance, which spawned great black writers such as Langston Hughes and fueled the music of the

Jazz Age, occurred as the result of the relocation of southern blacks to New York City. Yet another reason was the powerful influence Hollywood exerted on the movie-going public, and moviegoers there were. In 1922, 40 million attended films each week; by 1930, that number had risen to 115 million.

In art and fashion, the Exposition des Arts Decoratifs, held in Paris in 1925, gave birth to a style characterized by patterns of zigzag lines, hard-edged geometric forms, and a brilliant palette, often metallic, known as art deco. An elitist society emerged in New York City composed of actors, writers, and wealthy socialites, which glamorized cool sophistication and the sultry nighttime atmosphere of casinos and speakeasies. Illustrators such as John Held, Jr. created a distinctive, sparing style to capture the flapper, embodiment of femininity, with her short skirt and bobbed hair.

Mechanical inventions were saving time, but at the same moment making the passage of time go faster. With the increasing ubiquitousness of radios, automobiles, and especially, telephones, the postcard, which in 1910 could transfer a message to a neighboring town in as little as an hour or two, seemed less spontaneous. In 1919, one in 16 families had a car; this figure had risen to one in five by 1929. Likewise, radios became a fixture in most homes. There were 612 radio stations nationwide by 1930.

Left: Mexican border towns catered to the thirsty tourist trade during Prohibition years. Real photos of crowded streets lined with expensive automobiles, such as this view of the Juarez business district, offer mute testimony. The sign over the doorway reads, "OLD MEXICO CURIO SHOP. While You Are Still Sober Write Some Cards." Value $20-$25. Right: In between the real photos of small town brass bands and those of country and western groups lie the jazz ensembles of the 1920s. Most are elusive, though this photo of the Red Devil Orchestra is not. Value $10-$12.

Charlie Chaplin poses on this movie theatre promo for "The Heart Thief." A Chaplin quote appears on the reverse: "My mission...to make children happy, business men to forget their business troubles, the sick their pain, the old their age." Value: $15-$18.

CHARLES CHAPLIN

XMAS

CHRISTMAS SHEERS!

Not in miles of crowded store aisles could you find a lovelier gift. Rollins fine silk hosiery with its stylish lace tops, crystal clear silk, charming colors and its many features for long wear assure that your gift will endure for many months. A box of three pairs would be grand—for yourself, too.

Rollins Runstop Hosiery

THE PARISIAN

Mankato, Kansas

All Roads Lead To The BANCROFT
WORCESTER — MASSACHUSETTS

WHAT ARE THE WILD WIVES SAYING?

HEY!

Far left: Silk stockings were a status symbol in the '20s. The bold colors and art decoish graphics of this ad for Rollins Hosiery convey a hint of big city sophistication. Fairly scarce. Value $12-$15. Left: Automobiles and airplanes convey the modern traveler to the Bancroft Hotel from all angles. The text on reverse suggests that a newly mobile sales force was their target market: "No finer body of men exist than those who traverse the highways and by-ways in quest of the elusive order." Value $10-$12. Below center: This real photo of the Owl Club casino in Reno, NV, postmarked 1932, suggested that not everyone was impoverished during the Depression. Value $20-$25. Bottom: "What are the Wild Wives Saying?" asks this flapper comic. Value $2-$4.

In politics, postcards played an insignificant role in comparison with the campaigns of an earlier era, though Coolidge's campaign in 1924 could be the exception. "Silent Cal" may be remembered for having done less work and making fewer decisions than any other 20th century president, but he made up for it by posing for innumerable real photo postcards. Those showing him or his kin at their country home in Vermont appealed to the rural population, whose fortunes suffered a steady decline throughout the 1920s. It is quite possible that these frequently encountered cards were purposely intended to soften the image of a candidate whose maxim was, "the business of America is business."

By the early- to mid-1920s, the membership of the Ku Klux Klan had swollen to five million, its all-time high. Many members were rural dwellers uneasy with their increasingly precarious circumstances. Not just anti-black and anti-Semitic, the Klan's anti-immigrant stance had widespread appeal, especially when blanketed with a patriotic, fraternal facade. Laws passed in the 1920s lowered the flow of immigrants from approximately 800,000 in 1921 to well below 100,000 a year in the 1930s, with quotas based on nationality and favoring people of Western European descent. The immigration laws, together with financial scandals involving the leadership, weakened the appeal of the Klan as the decade wore on.

On a more upbeat note, the decade of the '20s was, more than anything else in the minds of many historians of popular culture, the era of the bona fide, larger-than-life hero. In 1927, Charles Lindbergh made his breathtaking transatlantic flight from New York to Paris. Not just a one-shot daredevil, Lindbergh flew many air mail runs in the late '20s, and is regarded as having done more to advance the cause of airmail and aviation in the United States than any other person. In the same year, Babe Ruth hit a record 60 home runs, which was to stand unbroken until 1961. Professional sports, especially baseball, football, and boxing, really took off in the '20s. Any postcards featuring stars of the era, such as Babe Ruth, Jack Dempsey, or Red Grange, are much sought after and highly valued.

John Coolidge at Plymouth "Listening in to Nomination of Calvin Coolidge at Cleveland Convention June 1924

Left: The radio had an impact on life in the 1920s similar to that of television on life in the 1950s. Here John Coolidge listens to Calvin's nomination, June 1924, on an early set. Real photo. Value $18-$20. Below left: There are several real photo views of Ku Klux Klan rallies and parades that turn up occasionally from Michigan or Maine in the early '20s. This one, of the 1925 Labor Day Celebration in Pontiac, MI, is unusual because the tent in the center has a banner stretched across it reading "HEADQUARTERS KKK." Value $50-$75. Below right: Charles Lindbergh himself flew this classic real photo view on the C.A.M. 2 airmail route between Chicago and St. Louis in 1928. Lindbergh was chief pilot on this route prior to his transatlantic flight. Value $30-$40.

The stock market crash in October 1929 heralded the close of an optimistic time of urban prosperity. The fortunes of average Americans in the early '30s grew ever more precarious as wages fell and millions of jobs disappeared. Postcards relating to the actual stock market crash are rare indeed, with good cause. Since it affected the country as a whole, there was no reason to publish disaster-type cards to let others outside the realm of misfortune know; while humorous cards were out of the question, considering the gravity of the situation. Easier to uncover are cards from the Depression urging people to make the best of things and look on the bright side.

The decade ends at a high point for the postcard collector, but a low point for American democracy—the march on Washington by the Bonus Army. Composed of thousands of destitute World War I vets, the Bonus Army converged on the Capitol in the summer of 1932. They had each been promised a $1000 war bonus, payable in 20 years. However, desperate circumstances led them to band together in an attempt to influence a congressional vote that would provide for immediate relief. In July the senate voted "No," but many marchers, having nowhere else to go, remained in a shantytown on the outskirts of the Capi-

Labor Day 1925 at Pontiac, Mich.

tol. On July 28 the army called out the tanks and tear gas and ran the squatters out of town. Three died, scores were injured, including women and children, while President Hoover commented, "Thank God we still have a government...that knows how to deal with a mob." Luckily for us, many fascinating postcards (see page one of this article), including at least one long set of printed views, record this black page in American history, just on the eve of the New Deal.

These ten years may not offer collectors the graphic diversity or plenitude of other decades, but with perseverance the old adage, "anything can be found on a postcard," may once again be proven true.

✳

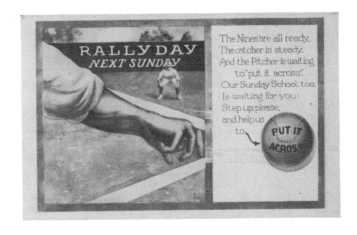

Top: Rally Day postcards—urging children to attend Sunday school—are commonly found used in the 1920s. An underrated collectible with some great designs and much diversity; this one crosses over into the sports field. Value $18-$20. Center: Real photos of World Series baseball teams are the Rolls-Royces of postcard collecting. While the view shown here of the 1928 Cardinals turned up in a quantity of several hundred a few years back, most have long since disappeared from dealers' stocks. Value $75-$100. Bottom: From a set of "Gloom Chaser" cards issued in the '30s comes this postal pep talk, which asserts "Yes...the fools are still buying new automobiles, and when enough of them get together, they'll tow America out of this mess." Value $8-$10.

George Gibbs grew up in Princeton, New Jersey, and graduated from Allegheny College in Meadville, Pennsylvania, in 1975 with degrees in History and English. He was subsequently employed as a photographer, medical abstracter, and surveyor for the National Trust for Historic Preservation before striking out on his own in 1982 to become a full-time postcard dealer. He now resides in Latham, New York.

GUESS I'M A COMMUNIST. I'VE GOT NO USE FOR THESE RICH GUYS WHO WANT TO GRAB EVERYTHING.

SOCIAL REVOLUTION IMPACTS SOCIETY

By Don Preziosi

With capitalism in disarray, the Depression was a time of desperation, which allowed Communism to gain a following during the first half of this decade. "Guess I'm A Communist," one of six comic designs from Manhattan Post Card Co., New York, NY, series #1476, takes a humorous look at an extremist viewpoint.

When I was asked to write about the years 1933 through 1942 in terms of social history and the development of the postcard, several things immediately sprang to my mind. In postcard terms it was obvious—LINENS! And for the social history of the period, I immediately thought of the Depression, F.D.R., world fairs, and World War II. Further reflection brought to mind other events, social developments, and aspects of popular culture that underwent significant changes during these years and had a lasting impact on American society. Some of these would include the repeal of prohibition; the impact of radio, Hollywood, comic strips, and comic books; gangsters and crime fighters; motels, nightclubs, and the American roadside; labor unions; glamour girls and pin-ups; and the streamlining of all modes of transportation and some types of architecture.

My own interest in this time period is a direct result of collecting postcards. Originally interested primarily in linen postcards (and older photo postcards), I soon became interested in any interesting postcards of the period, no matter what the production process. In fact it was soon apparent that certain categories would be almost exclusively covered by linen postcards (motels, humor, pin-ups, roadside restaurants), and other categories would almost never include linens (comic strips, auto advertising, political campaigns).

Linen postcards derive their name from the texture of the stock on which they are printed. It resembles the woven texture of linen cloth. As we shall soon see, this stock served both a technical and aesthetic purpose.

The inventor of the linen postcard was Curt Teich. Teich was a German immigrant who had been in the postcard business since 1905. His company was one of the largest producers of postcards in the United States, but with the onset of the Depression the postcard business began to decline.

Around 1930 Teich had developed a color printing process that would enable him to produce a more colorful looking card. The preparatory techniques were not new. A photographer would take a black and white photograph of the desired subject, and an enlargement would be made. Clients could indicate colors on a tissue overlay with the use of a numerical chart that Teich provided. A Teich artist would prepare a pencil sketch indicating any design and lettering additions along with

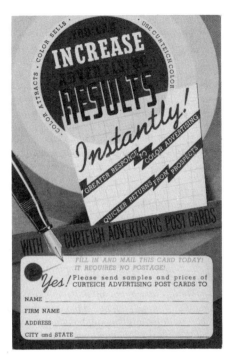

any revisions in the image itself. These revisions could be as innocuous as removing some telephone wires to as radical as eliminating and adding new backgrounds or foregrounds (more or fewer cars and people, depending on the desired effect), changing day scenes into night scenes, and enhancing the architectural aspects of a structure to make it far more appealing.

The Teich retouchers would then execute any and all changes on the black and white photographs. The airbrush was an essential tool for producing the subtle gradations of tone. Another artist could then do a watercolor mock-up of what the finished card might look like. Upon final approval, the material could then be turned over to the women on the Teich staff that specialized in creating the color overlays—all those wonderful reds, yellows, and blues (and combinations thereof) that linen cards are noted for—based on the sketch artist's and the client's information (sometimes the client would provide bits of carpet or other materials for particularly intricate patterns). Curt Teich used not only the standard four colors (red, yellow, blue, and black) to create his linen postcards, but also a fifth color which was the lighter blue that gave so many Teich linens an attractive look.

The final step was printing the separations on the new high-speed printing presses that Teich imported from Germany in order to improve inefficiency. Because the presses were now much faster, Teich needed to use a more absorbent paper stock that would enable the ink to dry faster. Thus the linen card was born. It changed the postcard business and catapulted the Curt Teich company to the leading position in the postcard industry for the next 20 years.

Probably the single most recognizable word that comes to mind when someone mentions the 1930s is "Depression." As a child of parents who grew up during the Depression, I became very aware that it was the defining event of the decade. It was not so much that my parents felt in any way deprived or restricted because of the Depression (my grandfathers were both self-employed), but

that the effects of the Depression had some psychological impact on anyone who lived through it. Large and frequent gatherings of my Italian-American relatives generated countless stories and reminiscences.

By 1933, 25 percent of the country was unemployed. Wages and industrial output had dropped roughly 50 percent since 1929. Forty million people were living in poverty. Those famous photographic images that come to mind are ones of despair—the bread lines, the scrawny farm woman and child, the Okies in their jalopies with all their worldly goods tied on, the dust bowl storms.

It is quite amazing that this cataclysmic turn of events in American life is scarcely documented on postcards of the period. (Note that I say "of the period." Some outstanding photos of the Depression have been reproduced in the last 20 years or so by modern postcard companies that specialize in photographic images.) I've encountered some comic cards that make reference to the hard times, and to some of Roosevelt's New Deal programs that were created to get the country out of the Depression.

Franklin Delano Roosevelt became the 32nd President of the United States on March 4, 1933. He was 51 years old and served as President for more than 12 years. Although born into wealth, he dedicated most of his life to public service. He was crippled by polio when he was 39, but obviously that did not deter him. He was admired for his courage, and had one of the most colorful personalities of our chief executives. During his presidency he became a champion of the "little" people, but the wealthy and the press were overwhelmingly anti-Roosevelt.

Roosevelt was a man of action, and his policies shaped the future of our country in a way that any one President rarely achieves. He took radical actions to deal with a desperate situation. There was a banking panic just weeks before his inauguration, so he closed all the banks and weeded out the "bad apples" to restore confidence in the system. He repealed prohibition, created the Social Security

✳ 29

system, and instituted a Good Neighbor Policy to create good will among our Latin American neighbors, but he is probably most associated with the creation of the New Deal.

The New Deal was a combination of federal relief money for those at the bottom of the economic ladder and new programs for economic planning on a national scale. Roosevelt craftily used his famous "fireside chats" (informal radio talks) to sell these programs to the public. A few of these "alphabet" agencies were:

N.R.A. (National Recovery Administration)—It basically regulated wages and hours, which strongly influenced prices. Business opponents called it "creeping socialism"; labor opponents said "business fascism."

C.C.C. (Civilian Conservation Corps)—It paid 2.5 million unemployed young people $30 each per month for projects of an ecological nature: reforestation, flood control, soil conservation, etc.

P.W.A. (Public Works Administration)—It provided funds for federally financed hospitals, bridges, transportation systems, tunnels, dams, public buildings, water and sewage systems, etc.

W.P.A. (Works Progress Administration)—This was the operational arm for the P.W.A. projects that provided jobs for people without work, and it also became a major patron of the arts, hiring thousands of writers, artists, photographers, composers, actors, and more to create, document, perform, and design for the public good.

Some of the other "alphabet" agencies that most of us are familiar with are the F.D.I.C. (Federal Deposit Insurance Corporation), the F.H.A. (Federal Housing Administration), the N.L.R.B. (National Labor Relations Board), the S.E.C. (Securities and Exchange Commission), and the T.V.A. (Tennessee Valley Authority).

It is possible to put together an interesting collection of F.D.R. postcards, but there are surprisingly few campaign postcards, considering that he ran for President four times. Some of the most interesting cards were issued by foreign countries during the World War II period. There are also some cards that are critical of Roosevelt's policies. In addition there are cards pertaining to the C.C.C., particularly campsites for the Corps (2.5 million young people away from home would surely be a prime market for postcards, though these are not common) and the T.V.A.

D esperate times provided a prime atmosphere for political extremists on the left and the right to expand their ranks. With capitalism in disarray, many intellectuals in New York and Hollywood were in sympathy with the growing Communist movement in the United States. At one time over seven million Americans were members of "fronts" that were set up to further the interests of many diverse groups. Similar thinking people worldwide also rallied around Moscow's fear that Hitler and the growing Nazi threat could jeopardize the Soviet Union (which at that time still had a favorable, or at least neutral, image in the West).

(Democracy in Action) F. D. R.

COPYRIGHT 1941, FRANK T. PERONE

Ironically, the downfall of American Communism was due primarily to Stalin himself. His ideological about-face in the incredible Nazi-Soviet pact of 1939 was very disillusioning to most American Communists, and they fled the party by the thousands.

A "Genuine Curteich-Chicago" issue for the Jersey Supply Company of Atlantic City, this linen postcard gives new meaning to the initials F.D.R.— Freedom-Defense-Recovery. Artwork by Frank T. Perone © 1941.

On the right, there were the activities of the Nazi-esque German-American Bund, which seemed to be centered in the metropolitan New York area. There was also Father Charles E. Coughlin, a popular priest who effectively used his radio broadcasts to form his own party, the National Union for Social Justice. He became known for his rabid anti-Roosevelt, anti-Communist, anti-union, and anti-Semitic attacks.

Some other colorful figures who held sway in the '30s were Dr. Francis Townsend, who had a novel economic retirement scheme, and Louisiana's infamous egotist, Huey Long, who was pushing his "Share the Wealth" program.

All of these fringe groups and characters can be found on postcards, but most of them are exceedingly rare.

T wo areas of popular culture in this period that immediately come to mind to many postcard collectors are the radio and Hollywood. There is no shortage of vintage postcards depicting the leading movie stars of the day. Radio postcards are not quite as common, perhaps because radio itself is not a visual medium, and many radio broadcasts were regional in nature.

As I've mentioned, radio was already being effectively used for political purposes. And it was becoming an increasingly important medium as a source of news. In the time frame of this article it certainly reached new heights in the live broadcasts of the rapidly unfolding events leading to our involvement in World War II. The cliche phrase "glued to their radios" perhaps best sums things up.

Radio was, however, primarily an entertainment

medium. Serial dramas, comedies, and a variety of musical programs dominated the airwaves. Add to that some sports and talk to round things out.

Hollywood movies of the era offered an escape from the dreary atmosphere of the Depression. Ironically millions (85 million a week!) of working class people flocked

to the theatres to see rich Hollywood stars sacrifice everything for the men/women they loved. Or perhaps to watch musical extravaganzas that cost millions to produce (while millions were living in poverty). Hollywood thrived while the rest of the country was struggling.

The movie stars were the uncrowned royalty of America, and none was more popular than the "princess" herself, Shirley Temple, the child star who was the top box office draw from 1935 to 1938. Some of the biggest box stars in the years from 1933 to 1942 were Will Rogers, Clark Gable, Mickey Rooney, Spencer Tracy, Tyrone Power, Robert Taylor, Joan Crawford, Bette Davis, Sonja Henie, and Fred Astaire and Ginger Rogers. But the list of memorable stars could probably go for a page or more, and if you like postcards, you can find them showing each of your favorite entertainers.

I won't even try to mention the great movies of the era, but I would be remiss if I did not mention "Gone With The Wind," the most expensive and most talked about movie of the period, that is still an icon of pop culture 53 years after its release.

And perhaps the ultimate escape from reality was the 1934 Walt Disney animated classic "Snow White and the Seven Dwarfs." This was Disney's first feature-length film, and it was a huge success. In spite of the growing popularity and success of the various Disney characters, it is difficult to find any Disney postcard material from this time period that was made in the U.S.A., but there are enough cards that were made for the European market to keep any collector busy.

Left: Radio postcards, such as this one from a Curteich "Radio Comics" series, are not very common. Right: James Montgomery Flagg, famous for Uncle Sam's "I Want YOU" poster, did the artwork for this "Lost Horizon" promotional postcard, which features a message from the movie's star, Ronald Colman, on the back.

It seems to me that there was an exposition or fair of major proportions almost every year from 1933 to 1940. In some years there were two. For postcard collectors the most significant ones are obviously the two biggest and most important, A Century of Progress Exposition in Chicago (1933-1934) and the New York World's Fair (1939-1940). The sheer quantity of postcards which these two expos generated would challenge even the most avid collector. Some of the other expos worth mentioning are the California-Pacific International Exposition (San Diego, 1935-1936) the Texas Centennial and the Pan-American Exposition (Dallas, 1936 and 1937), the Great Lakes Exposition (Cleveland, 1937), and the Golden Gate International Exposition (San Francisco, 1939-1940).

A Century of Progress, which was conceived to mark the 100th anniversary of Chicago, was notable for several reasons.

Architecturally it was vastly different from the plaster of paris pomposity of earlier U.S. fairs, and its highly acclaimed exhibits of science and industry were housed in much more utilitarian buildings. Financially it was a success in spite of the fact that it was being held in the midst of a serious depression. Whereas almost all fairs of this caliber rack up huge debts, this one actually paid back its bondhold-

Borden's Dairy World of Tomorrow highlighted Elsie the Cow as their star attraction at the New York World's Fair (1939-1940). Artwork by Walter Early.

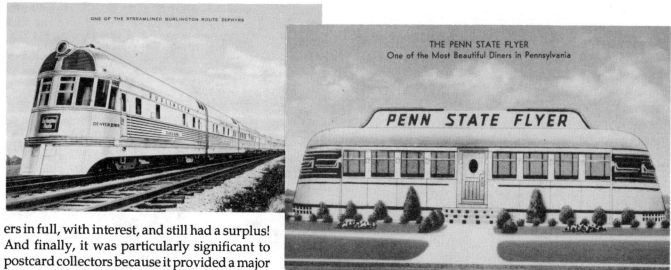

THE PENN STATE FLYER
One of the Most Beautiful Diners in Pennsylvania

ers in full, with interest, and still had a surplus! And finally, it was particularly significant to postcard collectors because it provided a major showcase for the new linen-style postcards, and was probably, in my opinion, instrumental in making the linen cards a success.

The New York World's Fair was the biggest and costliest international exposition to date. It commemorated the 150th anniversary of the inauguration of George Washington as the first president of the United States. It was billed as "the World of Tomorrow," and had as its architectural symbols the Trylon (a triangular obelisk) and the Perisphere (a large ball-like structure). It introduced to the general public new technological advances such as television, nylon, air conditioning, and robots, but it also featured artistic expression with all of the modern architecture, and massive murals and sculptures by the leading talents of the day. And the amusement section catered to more pedestrian (and occasionally prurient) tastes.

There was literally something for everyone, and much of it was documented by postcards. I would estimate that there are several scores of sets and series (some over 100 cards long) in addition to a hundred or more individual cards.

In retrospect, the "look" of the New York World's Fair was perhaps the apogee of the streamlining trend in America rather than a portent of "the world of tomorrow." The 1930s have been referred to as the "Streamlined Decade." Streamlining had as it roots a functionalism based on scientific principles of aerodynamics and hydrodynamics: smooth surfaces and transitional curves offered less resistance to air and water. Although it was not simply an aesthetic development, the impetus for redesigning some products was certainly motivated by the desire for a new look. For the same reasons that Curt Teich came up with a new look for postcards in reaction to declining sales, other manufacturers also recognized a need to redesign their product if they expected to generate sales in the midst of the Depression. The impact on some architecture and much industrial design is quite remarkable in contrast to the prior boxy, hard-edged look, and nowhere was it more obvious than in the field of transportation.

Automobile engineers were interested in aerody-

namic techniques decades earlier, but these prototypes were never intended for production-line vehicles. It would take 20 years for public tastes to mesh with scientific principles. (Probably the most famous of the 1930s "streamline" designers, Raymond Loewy followed his own MAYA—most advanced yet acceptable—principle for product design.) The most renowned production car in the streamlining of automobiles was the 1934 Chrysler Airflow. One would only have to look at any automobile manufactured just a few years earlier to marvel at the transition—built-in headlights, curved front, sloped back, wheelcovers, and minimal external protuberances.

The look in locomotives went from the dawning-of-the-Industrial-Age clunkiness of the black steam engine to the sleek and colorful styling of the Zephyrs, Comets, Rockets, Electroliners, and Streamliners (of course!) that took over the rails in the 1930s.

On the seas the most radical external design changes showed up on car ferries, while the larger ocean liners would reflect streamlining influences in their interior design.

In the air, the "flying boats" and "Clippers" incorporated both hydrodynamic and aerodynamic improvements into an aesthetically and commercially successful mode of transportation. However, the first fully streamlined commercial airplane was the Douglas DC-2.

There is an abundance of postcards that can be found to represent the streamlining of our transportation industry. The airline, railroad, and shipping industries all

Streamlining is synonymous with the 1930s. Left: One of the streamlined Burlington Route Zephyrs. An E.C. Kropp Company card published by the Ottumwa News Service, Ottumwa, IA. Right: Roadside diners were a popular topic for linen postcards and remain highly collectible today as well. The Penn State Flyer, "One of the Most Beautiful Diners in Pennsylvania," has a streamlined look all its own on this Edward I. Plottle Co. advertising postcard.

issued promotional postcards that were generally available free to their customers when on board. Likewise auto manufacturers, through their dealerships, offered postcards or mailed out postcards to potential customers. These often added sales and/or price pitches to the attractive illustrations of their vehicles.

In the field of architecture the single most significant group of postcards that show the effects of streamlining are those of the art deco district of Miami Beach.

The bright colors and airbrushed look of linen postcards made them the perfect medium to lure the Depression-weary public to this vacation resort. Additional examples of streamlined architecture can be found on some cards depicting the public buildings (stations, court houses, etc.) built under the auspices of the P.W.A. and on the roadside structures (diners, tourist courts, drive-ins, etc.) that were rapidly being built to serve the interests of the ever-increasing traveling public.

The availability of affordable automobiles, the expanding highway system, and the steady growth and interest of westward development necessitated the growth of businesses that could cater to the gas, food, and lodging needs of this new traveling public. This would have a major social impact and, not surprisingly, have a significant impact on the types of postcards that would be sent and saved.

Prior to the 1930s, the facilities between cities and towns were few and far between. Campsites that had sprung up near small towns eventually gave way to tourist courts which were updated by the motel (short for motor-hotel); roadside restaurants and diners provided cheap meals; gas stations replaced the pumps by the general store; and cheap roadside attractions promoted to capture a piece of the roadside dollar. Restaurants and motels offered free postcards to their customers and would often mail them for free, too. These needs kept the postcard business hopping, and keep today's roadside collectors happy in pursuit of the cards that document this uniquely American phenomena. Route 66, diners, and drive-ins are all hot topics today.

On September 1, 1939, Germany invaded Poland, and history was once more on an altered course. Germany continued its march through Europe and within only a year had Great Britain as its only major obstacle and Italy as an ally. On December 7, 1941, Japan bombed Pearl Harbor, and the U.S. was drawn into the war with Great Britain, China, and the Soviet Union as its major allies against the Axis powers (Germany, Italy, Japan, and six others).

Thousands of different postcards were made relating to this turn of events. Naturally there was a great need for the millions of people in the military to send inexpensive cards to friends and family. Cards of military bases, military life, military vehicles and aircraft, and military humor are in abundant supply for today's collectors. There are also scores of different propaganda-type cards. There are surprisingly few cards of any sort of combat, and not too much other than comic cards on how the home front was dealing with the situation.

This is where we end this decade of postcard history. Bloody battles were raging on several continents in the greatest, costliest, deadliest, and most destructive war the world has ever known; Roosevelt was elected to an unprecedented third term; and the country was on the rebound from the worst depression it has ever known.

✳

A soldier stands guard at the Camp Edwards Anti-Aircraft Artillery Training Center in Massachusetts. This, a Christmas greeting most likely issued for soldiers to send to family and friends, is just one of thousands of postcards issued during World War II.

Don Preziosi and his wife, Newly, are full-time dealers in vintage postcards. They also publish and distribute contemporary postcards on progressive political issues. From 1983 to 1988 Don was a monthly columnist and occasional feature writer for *Postcard Collector*, specializing in the Linen Era. They live in Mendham, NJ, with their children, Nick and Susanna, and Roogie the cat.

POSTCARDS
EXPERIENCE
COLLECTIBILITY
UPSWING

By Lewis Baer

As the popularity cycle rose for postcards, exchanges became an integral part of the hobby. Shown here in postcard form is a list of guidelines, established by "Post Card Collectors News" editor Bob Hendricks for the Post Card Collectors Club of America, defining the proper etiquette to follow when trading with others.

Postcards recorded the Second World War and its finale, but not with the fervor that they had chronicled World War I, the war to end all wars. The public no longer needed postcards for a visual record of world events. Daily newspapers were filled with illustrations; magazines such as *Life* and *Look* published high quality photo stories each week; and the movies brought the news to life between every cartoon and feature film.

There were some excellent photo cards made during World War II, such as the "London Under Fire" series that showed the destruction and encouraged the citizenry with quotes signed "The Prime Minister." Postcards had been a popular medium for propaganda throughout Europe in the early war years, but became increasingly scarce as countries were overrun.

In this country, too, postcard supplies were restricted by the war effort. In order to conserve material, the War Production Board placed direct limitations on the manufacture of illustrated postcards. They were still popular though, and plenty were published. Those used for correspondence often received a censor's cachet before they were delivered.

Most of the war cards published here would

seem to be comics, a class of cards often scorned by early collectors. But military humor was a popular theme, and many linens featured scowling Hitlers and Tojos being "flushed," or smiling GIs waving at WACs. Popular cartoon characters went to war on postcards, and George Lichty of "Grin and Bear It" renown produced a comical postcard commentary. "Private Breger" cards

Devastation wrought by the war is evident on this example from the "London Under Fire" postcard series.

PRIVATE BREGER
By Sgt. Dave Breger

"I WOULD hafta deliver a message to the Colonel when his orderly is sick!"

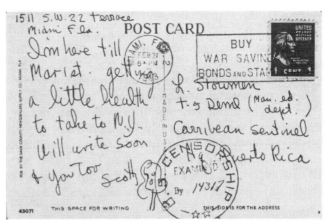

Above: Postcards sent during World War II to family and friends in military service often passed through the hands of a censor. Left: Comic cards, such as those in Dave Breger's "Private Breger" series, carried the popular military humor theme during the war.

were the most typically American of this humorous genre. Dave Breger, who went on to become a Second Lieutenant by the war's end, created the character based on his own experiences. These lighthearted cards exemplified the American traditions of volunteerism and patriotism tempered with feckless naivete. The artist continued publishing after the war with a "Breger on Vacation" series.

During the '40s and early '50s, many events took place that drastically changed human existence for the 50 years to follow. The development of penicillin and the birth of the atomic age were the two most widely felt. It was a time of dramatic change for postcards, and the postcard collecting hobby in the United States, as well.

The death of the penny postcard on January 1, 1952, was mourned by collectors and correspondents throughout the land when the postage rate was raised. The increase had been tried before—in 1928—but only on picture postcards. Revenues declined as a result, and embarrassed officials quickly returned the rate

Commercial real photos, such as this one of the Pacific Highway over the Umpqua River in Oregon, usually cost 15 cents each in the early 1950's

to one cent. This time there was to be no reprieve, in spite of pleas before Congress to spare this "American institution." New cards on the rack were commonly priced at three linens for a dime and 15 cents each for commercial real photos. Now, postage on them—and government postals—would cost two cents a piece.

Another major development during the years 1943-1952 was the beginning of the chrome postcard era.

Several publishers, most notably the McKee Company, had experimented with postcards printed in life-like tones using photographic originals, the four-color process, and an offset press. None of these early cards were well received until 1939 when Union Oil Company published the first widely distributed chromes. The fronts, which featured scenic views of the western states and provinces, were almost-natural full color, glossy reproductions. They looked just like photographs. Issued again in 1940 and 1941, they were instantly popular with collectors. During the war there was little tourism and no need to advertise gasoline products, and the next Union Oils didn't appear until 1947. By that time the trend toward chromes had taken firm hold with other publishers. Union Oil put out three more issues, 1948, 1950, and 1955, to make seven sets in all ranging from 51 to 288 cards per set. Many were re-issues of earlier cards. There

were also three Canadian sets—1939, 1940, and 1945—of 12 cards each.

The credit for perfecting the technology behind chrome postcards goes largely to Mike Roberts and his "Wesco Color Cards," which for years bore the slogan "Reproduced from natural color photograph" or "from Kodachrome." The management of the Curt Teich Company, the one-time world's largest volume producer of postcards, maintained that chromes were only a passing fad and that linens would return to favor. Teich did eventually switch over to chrome production, but too late. The company was never to regain its historic share of the market. This new style of cards became popular after the war, and the beginning of the Chrome Era is generally accepted as 1945. Since that time nearly all commercially produced cards throughout the world have been chromes.

Today two-cent postage seems ludicrous, and chromes are viewed as only one phase in the century of U.S. picture postcard history. But developments in the '40s and early '50s have had a resounding effect on the postcard collecting hobby of today.

From the time postcards first appeared, their popularity for collecting has risen and fallen in cycles. In the early '40s the hobby was just entering an upswing that was to last more than a decade. Much of this impetus was created in the pages of *Post Card Collectors News*, a magazine first published in 1943 by Bob Hendricks, a disabled veteran. Unlike other postcard magazines which were little more than lists of names for exchanging cards through the mail, Hendricks published four pages of news about postcards, and his editorials spurred increased interest in the hobby. At the time, most hobbyists were general collectors and all postcards were considered of equal value. They were traded on a card for card basis. Through Hendricks' pages, collectors began to discover each other and to come together to form local clubs, to learn about their cards, to define areas of interest, and to establish values as a basis for exchanging cards.

Hendricks reflected on his motivation a few years later when he wrote that he had "a great interest in my card pals and their collections," and he believed collectors would enjoy reading about others in the hobby. He was right, as 500 copies of his first issue were quickly distributed, and by 1947 he had 1300 subscribers. It was that year that Hendricks took over a similar magazine from Kansas City. It came with 2500 subscribers and several hundred dollars of debt. To further complicate his life, he became editor for the newly formed Southern California Postcard Club.

Hendricks' convoluted publishing career is difficult to follow. It was never a financial success. For years he worked two jobs to keep his magazines afloat, and there would often be long breaks between issues. Subscribers were unclear as to just which magazines they were paying for, and subscriptions would be ex-

Bob Hendricks' artistry appeared on a number of postcards. This one was intended for use as a maximum card.

tended to make up for missing issues. It must have confused Hendricks as well, for when he died in 1962, he left behind two barrels full of unopened mail.

However frustrating his publishing ventures may have been, they allowed him to continue his editorial pursuits. Hendricks believed that postcards were more than just pictures to be traded back and forth. He came to recognize that they were individual documents, and he encouraged collectors to study their cards and to share their knowledge. This project started off slowly. In the early '40s, he published mostly checklists for large letters, Union Oils, and Detroits. Later came research on publishers and the never ending study of postcard artists.

Hendricks was a staunch believer in local clubs. He liked the chumminess of personal contact and the one-on-one exchange of postcards and information. In July 1947 he wrote about the local clubs that had already been formed: the Cleveland club in 1945, the Metropolitan Postcard Collectors of New York, the Southern California group, and the Magnolia chapter of the Post Card Collectors Club of America in New Orleans. In 1948 a Wilmington, Delaware, chapter and Chicago's Windy City club would be added to the list. Hendricks continued his editorial lobbying for local groups over the next dozen years.

Hendricks also encouraged artists to produce new cards which he promoted through his publication. The stylish serigraphed cards made by Dubosclard in the later '50s were a result of Hendricks' efforts, as were the many chromes of mouth artist Nyla Thompson and her paintings. Hendricks brought Dwig to local club meetings, and also cartoonist Bob Petley. Both were subjects of editorials and articles.

The editor had artistic talents of his own and designed more than 60 postcards in editions of 1000 each. One of his earliest cards, P-3, was a statement of ethics for all collectors (see page one of this article). His own artwork was featured on several cards, like the Edgar Allan Poe maxi-card, P-22-49, shown here without the commemorative stamp and cancel that would fulfill the maxi requirements.

Hendricks reproduced historic photos on postcards and created a few rarities along the way. Card P-60-53 was originally published as "Casablanca Conference" and identified the participants as De Gaulle, F.D.R., and Churchill. The error was caught and a new card issued

CASABLANCA CONFERENCE, January 14-26, 1943

Charles De Gaulle   *Franklin D. Roosevelt*   *Winston Churchill*

Above: One of only about ten error cards issued by Hendricks, it features the wrong time, the wrong place, and the wrong leader! Below left: Postcard issued by the Windy City Postcard Club upon Hendricks' induction into their Postcard Hall of Fame. Below right: Snapshot of Hendricks at a local postcard club meeting. Photo courtesy Bob Wilkie.

with the same number and photo but now labeled "Quebec Conference" and with Mackenzie King correctly named. In a letter to a friend, Hendricks mentions the error: "Had a new card made. Don't throw the other one away. Only about ten of them got out. It will be a novelty...will have to destroy the balance of the Casablanca cards."

Believing the hobby needed a more dignified name, Hendricks encouraged another collector to delve into word origins and create a new term. The result: Deltiology.

When Hendricks learned that some hobbyists were studying the history of postcards, he gave them much publicity and support. He called J.R. Burdick's 1946 first edition of *The American Card Catalog* "a splendid piece of research analysis," although it dealt mostly with trade cards and contained less than two pages on postcards. Burdick went on to compile a second edition, with more than a dozen pages on postcards, followed by a handbook on the Detroit Publishing Company and an in-depth study of Pioneer cards, which is still a major research source.

In 1946 another disabled vet, W. Bourcy-Beckley, joined the hobby. He was disappointed to find no guidebook to help him learn more about postcards. So, with Hendricks' prodding, Beckley researched and wrote *The Post-Card Handbook*, which first appeared in 1949. He attempted to organize the enormous field of postcards into two broad and overlapping categories: Type A, manufacturing processes, which included printing methods and shapes, sizes, and novelties; and Type B, subject matter.

A later edition included Type C, publishers. The handbook was plagued with inconsistencies, but it was only a first attempt, and in a review the remarkable story of the book was revealed. "The printer had lost the manuscript, and Bourcy-Beckley sat down at the printer's desk and wrote the entire edition from memory!"

According to postcard scholar Rita Nadler, who contributed to Beckley's second edition, the *Handbook* was important because "it was widely circulated on the east and west coasts, and it really got collectors thinking."

From the late '40s on, a continuing dialogue on values appeared in Hendricks' magazines. "What are postcards worth?" "Surely no more than the three to five cents they cost new." "But what about the 'rare' cards which were identified in Beckley's book?" Suddenly, some postcards which had all been a penny a piece were "worth" a nickel, others a quarter, and a few scarce Detroits as much as five dollars!

Hendricks retired in 1959 as the hobby entered a cyclical lull. A few years later the Windy City club published a postcard honoring him as the first inductee into its Postcard Hall of Fame. The photo was the same as had appeared in his magazines since 1943. I think a snapshot of him from Bob Wilkie's collection is more the way Hendricks should be remembered—at a local club meeting, gavel in hand, surrounded by collectors and postcards.

✳

Author's Note: Thanks to Jonah Shapiro, Rita Nadler, Roy Nuhn, Bob Wilkie, and Matt Infeld for sharing their files and their knowledge to make this article possible.

Lewis Baer lives in Northern California where he collects goats on postcards. He has written many articles on the hobby and the people in it, in the hope of sharing their insights and enthusiasm with collectors everywhere.

BOB HENDRICKS
(1918-1962)

✳ 37

Traveling Back to the Fabulous Fifties

And what better way to go than in this pair of 1958 DeSotos—one for Mom and Dad and a miniature model for the kids. From the collection of John Baeder. © Fotofolio, New York, NY.

By Jennifer Henderson

*You're traveling through another dimension,
a dimension not only of sight and sound but of mind;
a journey into a wondrous land whose boundaries are that
of imagination. That's the signpost up ahead—
your next stop...the 1950s.*

Welcome to the Fabulous Fifties on postcards! The 1950s—actually 1953 to 1962 in the context of this centennial volume—was a time when postcards, sent for pennies, sold us on new items to purchase, on new places to visit, and on new ways to dine. It was a time when television and travel invited Americans to consume and keep on consuming. It was a

"The Crowning of Her Majesty Queen Elizabeth in Westminster Abbey." Published by Raphael Tuck & Sons Ltd.

time when the spacious family car transported Dad, Mom, and the kids to new eating and entertainment experiences.

Television in the "Twilight Zone" of the '50s grew into a major industry. Although TV debuted in the United States in 1927, it wasn't until the late 1940s that the public could buy their first clunky, small-screen sets. In 1950, only nine percent of American households owned black and white TVs; eight years later, eight out of ten homes had them. Gradually, television assumed a pivotal role, especially in the areas of advertising and information.

In 1953, America inaugurated a war hero named Dwight D. "Ike" Eisenhower, who was the first U.S. President to use television to get elected. A new magazine for channel-chasing, *TV Guide*, went on sale during the week of April 3rd to help the recently converted catch news about the muck in Korea or the McCarthy hearings. A major event, the coronation of Queen Elizabeth II on June 2nd, was not only broadcast on television for the world to see, but also preserved on a black and white Tuck postcard.

Millions of viewers caught the antics of Lucy, Desi, and the Mertzes in their city apartments, at their suburban home, and as they drove off for vaca-

tion adventures. Other comfortable fictional families set an example on "Leave It to Beaver," "Ozzie and Harriet," and "Lassie." In TV Land, Donna Reed was such a calm mother and Robert Young such an understanding father that life's situations always ended smoothly and quickly on the "watching box." After school the kids tuned into cartoons—"Howdy Doody" and the "Mickey Mouse Club."

A national unity was developing, encouraged by television ads that trained Americans to be informed consumers by eating, wearing, and buying the same "new and improved" brand-name products. Nowhere did the slogan, "It pays to advertise" fit better than on television, where businesses prospered with such rhyming jingles as "See the U.S.A. in your Chevrolet" or "You can tell it's Mattel, it's swell."

Of all the foods introduced during the 1950s, none better conveys the era than TV dinners. They are modern, fast, and convenient. One USDA survey determined that economic conditions were favorable for American housewives to spend additional money on time- and effort-saving processed foods. For 98 cents, the C.A. Swanson & Sons' TV Dinners were ready to serve (after only a brief stay in the oven) on their own aluminum tray neatly divided into three compartments that kept the turkey and cornbread stuffing separated from the mashed sweet potatoes and the buttered peas. Swanson's "TV Turkey Dinner" was originally introduced in October 1953 to a lunchtime gathering of 150 food writers in Chicago. Since the overall response was so positive, the company started mass production immediately. This marked the first time that a complete frozen meal was to be distributed nationally.

In 1955, Roy Rogers was the biggest gun in the field of human celebrity endorsers. Although Disney characters actually topped the list, Rogers was a favorite radio, TV, and movie singing star with a popular wife, horse, dog, sidekick, jeep, and ranch. "The Roy Rogers Show" ran from 1951 to 1957 and stimulated sales for his line of clothes and accessories to make junior cowpokes resemble their horse-

Left: Lucy, Desi, and friends are off on another auto escapade. Reproduction by Hallmark Cards, Inc. of a © 1954 photo by CBS Inc. Right: The future of cooking for the '50s homemaker. © The American Postcard Co.

back hero, like on the advertising chrome for Pauker's official Roy Rogers sweaters shown below. In the November 15, 1954, issue of *Life*, Rogers bought a four-page Christmas insert to promote his diverse line of merchandise: cowboy and cowgirl outfits, holster sets, kerchiefs, frontier shirts, leather jackets, skirts, chaps, vests, sweatshirts, jeans, denim jackets, flashlights, raincoats, archery sets, bedspreads and drapes ("Roy Rogers and Trigger in distinctive colors"), lunchboxes, belts, gloves, Viewmaster reels, bedroom slippers and "ranchjamas," clocks, Roy and Dale Evans hats, and miniature Nellybelle jeeps big enough for little cowhands to drive.

Shiny automobiles were showcased on television, in magazines, and on postcards from local dealerships. President Eisenhower's idea for an interstate highway system, based on Germany's limited-access autobahns, inspired cross-country jaunts. Extravagant new cars, especially models with fantastic fins like the 1958 DeSoto and cheap gasoline, inspired driving with "no particular place to go." However, there were always the drive-ins.

Drive-in restaurants originally appealed to those who wanted to eat in the spacious comfort of their cars. Carhops delivered Cokes and fries on a tray attached to the car window, usually on the driver's side. Instead of

Advertising postcard for Pauker's official Roy Rogers sweaters.

having to pop coins in the jukebox inside, you could leave the AM car radio on, blaring out the latest Top Forty releases from Elvis Presley, Jerry Lee Lewis, the Everly Brothers, or Bill Haley and His Comets. But eating in the car was such an unprecedented idea that people had to be convinced about the practicality of dining curbside.

Roy Kroc built his first McDonald's franchise in 1955; by the time the 500 millionth hamburger had been sold in 1961, Kroc had bought out the McDonald brothers. Competitors for burger dollars included Whataburger, Red Barn, Jack in the Box, A&W (with Mama, Papa, and Baby burgers perfect for all members of the family), Burger King, White Castle, White Tower, Big Boy, and Burger Chef, which in 1959 mailed out government postal cards with coupons good for a free milk shake printed on the back. Postcards of this type are rare since the recipient generally redeems the coupon, after which they're discarded by the company issuing them.

For so many families with kids, drive-in movies proved the ideal choice for an evening out. No babysitter or parking fees were required; admission was cheap; and everyone could watch from the car. At intermission, there was food available and swings, slides, and jungle gyms for anyone with too much energy to sit still. No matter that the sound came out of squawk boxes or that the film might not be a first-run hit, drive-ins were so popular that eventually even Marilyn Monroe movies were featured there.

Sleepy drivers needed a place to rest, so motels and motor inns sprang up along the country's roadways. The Holiday Inn chain started in 1952 but did not get off the ground until the following year. Huge and well-lit, their sign served as a beacon to motorists. Tired from a day on the road, families pulled into a Holiday Inn, confident that there would be a TV, swimming pool, free postcards in the desk drawer, and that kids under 12 stayed free. Holiday Inns were big on franchising; New York Yankees great Mickey Mantle operated the Holiday Inn in Joplin, Missouri.

In 1959, the Burger Chef in Waukegan, IL, used postcards to advertise a free milk shake (15-cent value!) as a get acquainted offer.

The perfect destination, Disneyland, opened in 1955. Everything, even the conception of outer space, matched the wonderment that travel and television helped develop. Honoring a '50s fad, the flying saucer ride in Tomorrowland allowed each "guest [to] pilot his own ship in free flight, above the ground." In *Populuxe*, Thomas Hine writes that "Disneyland was the first place ever conceived simultaneously with a television series, and the geography of Disneyland was known by millions of people all over America even before the place existed."

Marilyn Monroe starred in "The Seven Year Itch" in 1954, during the time that drive-in movies were a popular choice for family entertainment.

Disneyland issued hundreds of different postcards, as did assorted tourist attractions: alligator farms, Paul Bunyan statues, petrified forests, and the like. For such publishers as Dexter Press, H.S. Crocker, Curteichcolor, Mike Roberts, Plastichrome, Hannau Color, and Tichnor Brothers, travel fueled a need for 1950s postcards. Hotels and motels, airlines and bus lines, gas stations, and cafes, diners, and restaurants issued free postcards to spread the word about their great food or service. The mobile populace wanted to write home or remember places visited, and postcards have always proved the ideal souvenir.

Advertising postcard for Mickey Mantle's Holiday Inn in Joplin, MO.

Factories that conducted tours—as diverse as Kellogg's cereals, Chesterfield cigarettes, and Italian Swiss Colony wines—were so eager to have tourists send postcards to their friends and families they would not only distribute the cards and provide a place to write them, but pay for the postage as well.

Besides views of scenic interest, 1950s postcards featured things to buy. Following the Second World War, America's economy boomed, and with so many families moving to the suburbs, there were plenty of purchases needed to fill these brand new homes. Between October 1954 and July 1956, "Feather Your Nest" played daily on NBC and offered couples the chance to win prizes for their homes by answering questions. This and programs of its type helped to educate, especially the housewife able to watch during the day, about new, efficient, and beautiful things for her home. "Viewers saw a continuously changing panorama of home furnishings," one reviewer wrote, "which made them more home beautifying-conscious and concurrently, more brand name-conscious." Such sponsors as Drexel Furniture used postcards to keep their dealers excited about the show and to explain new sales ideas.

Direct mail merchandising also generated postcards as retailers might send out cards advertising the latest style in refrigerators, aluminum pans, bedroom sets, barbecue grills, swimming pools, or lawn mowers. Most of these glossy full-color photographic postcards presented their wares in fine detail, but there were sloppy cards with fuzzy images or colors that appeared too dark. Oftentimes, the postcard corners were rounded.

A 1954 publicity photograph of "The Honeymooners," © VIP Corp., reprinted by The American Postcard Company Inc.

Recent publications include books filled with oversized, perforated postcards that give a flavor of early rock and roll and Roger Corman-type "B" movies, but those pub-

A '50s version of the flying saucer had its place in Disneyland's Tomorrowland. © Walt Disney Productions.

lished now evolved from feelings of present-day nostalgia rather than reproductions of postcards past. However, Quantity Cards of San Francisco has rescued and reprinted many funky chromes so that modern-day racks can feed this yearning for the '50s.

Postcard clubs played an important role with collectors in the 1950s. The earliest of the lot, such as the Metropolitan Post Card Collectors Club and All States Hobby Club, were started on the east coast and involved monthly meetings, special exhibits, bourses, and newsletters which might advertise round robin trades. A few clubs published official postcards, and some were issued in conjunction with postage stamp organizations. A real beauty was published for the November 27, 1955, meeting of the Connecticut Post Card Club, which welcomed the Connecticut Philatelic Society. This card (right) features a gold medallion of President Lincoln embossed over an American flag along with a canceled four-cent, Lincoln postage stamp.

Optimism and prosperity swelled in the early 1960s. President Kennedy's inauguration, combined with America's first manned space flight and the

The Connecticut Post Card Club
welcomes
The Connecticut Philatelic Society
Sunday, November 27, 1955

Seattle World's Fair in 1962, gave a false sense that everything was and ever would be right with the world. The '50s ended when postal zones gave way to zip codes, when well-endowed Barbie dolls beat out the Mouseketeers, and when the Beatles landed on Ed Sullivan. For the 1950s, the honeymoon was really over when brash bus driver Ralph Kramden was run off the road by that hot Corvette on "Route 66."

✳

Jennifer Henderson survived the 1950s by going along with her family on long drives across the U.S.A. from Miami to Disneyland to Seattle with lots of Holiday Inns in-between. If there's anything more interesting to collect, study, and write about than postcards, she has yet to find it. Her current passion, recipe postcards, keeps her busy sifting, sorting, and sending away for new editions to appear in the *Cookin' with Postcards* catalog.

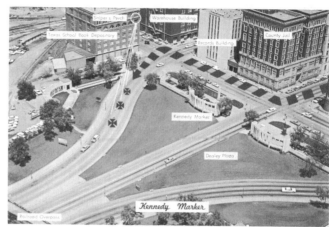

CONFLICT & CONTRASTS PERMEATE THE TIMES

By Diane Allmen

Conflicts in the 1960s brought about several assassinations. This view of Dallas, Texas, site of the Kennedy assassination, is numbered 21999-C, printed by Dexter Press, and published by All-Tom Corporation. Several similar viewcards with overprinted identifying descriptions were issued by various distributors. They are very common in standard, continental, and oversize.

Looking back on the decade 1963 to 1972, I view it as <u>my</u> decade for nostalgia. For me, these years were filled with new and challenging activities and experiences. I was a student in Ann Arbor, then got a job in Chicago, protested the war, and spent my free time pursuing my hobby...photography. I didn't collect postcards at the time, but I actively bought and used them. Now, as an avid postcard collector, many of those mailed to relatives have been returned to me. (I even have a postally-used real photo that I made in my own darkroom.) Reviewing key events of the decade evokes many memories. Postcards make these memories tangible and can be associated in some way with almost every event. Selecting representative examples for this article has been a nostalgic trip back!

The majority of postcards from the decade 1963 through 1972 were standard-size, 3-1/2"x5-1/2", chromes (printed by the four color half-tone process from color photographs and finished with a shiny coating). In the U.S., five major postcard printers and dozens of smaller companies produced most of the work. They manufactured both viewcards for local

distributors as well as advertising cards for individual clients. All of the companies assigned unique stock numbers to the postcards for rapid identification. By mastering these stock number codes and sequences, collectors can often determine the age of a postcard or when it was first issued.

Curt Teich of Chicago was one of the largest postcard printing companies during this decade. In 1963 Teich's stock numbers were prefixed with "3D," in 1964 with "4D," in 1965 with "5D," and so forth through the '60s; in 1970 the stock number prefix was "0E," in 1971 "1E," and in 1972 "2E." Thus, the code becomes obvious: the letters "D" and "E" represent the decades 1960 and 1970 respectively, and the numeral a particular year within the decade.

Dexter Press of West Nyack, New York, another major postcard printer, had sequentially-assigned stock numbers. Two years ago, my business partner, Dave Long, and I purchased the postcard archives of Dexter Press. We've only examined a fraction of this two-million card acquisition, but can estimate when many cards were issued by their stock numbers. In

1963, stock numbers started at approximately 58000-B and continued over the next year or so to 99999-B; they began again at zero with a "C" suffix and by the early '70s the "C" series was completed through 99999-C and the "D" series had begun.

The chrome postcards of the printer Koppel, of Hawthorne, New Jersey, were characterized by a bold "K" over a horizontal diamond shape located in the lower left corner of the back. Sequentially-assigned stock numbers had reached the 11,000s by 1969.

Mike Roberts of San Francisco and Plastichrome of Boston were two additional major printers of standard-size chromes in the 1960s.

The cost of mailing a postcard in the U.S. increased over this decade. Postcard postage rates were raised in one-cent increments from four cents in 1963 to six cents by 1972.

Postcard clubs for exchanging information and postcards attracted nationwide memberships in the 1960s. Local members usually met monthly and often produced periodic newsletters. In addition to trading postcards, a major activity was compiling checklists of local postcard publishers. Clubs such as the Maple City (northern Indiana); Windy City (Chicago); Metropolitan (New York City); and Rhode Island Post Card Club shared checklists and exchanged newsletters. Many club members worked on completing their collections of Union Oil cards (series of chrome views issued by Union Oil Company in 1939, 1940, 1941, 1947, 1948, 1950, and 1955).

American society during the decade 1963 through 1972 can be characterized as one of great contrasts and much conflict. It was a time of fear, gloom, and repression—Anti-Communism and the Cold War. There was also high optimism—the War on Poverty and advances in civil rights for non-white Americans. There was intense distrust of the status quo. It was challenged on campus, in prison, in the inner cities, and even at political conventions. The decade was marked by political assassinations: John F. Kennedy (1963); Malcolm X (1965); Robert Kennedy and Martin Luther King (1968). And political arrogance: Watergate. Some people volunteered for the Peace Corps or VISTA, while others dropped out on acid or marijuana, moved to communes, and listened to Janis (Joplin) and Jimi (Hendrix).

Postcards documenting this social conflict and social change, produced at the time, are difficult to find and quite desirable. Modern postcards produced in the 1980s and 1990s are beginning to recover this lost decade. Of special interest are the black and white photographs of events from the '60s published by Fotofolio and Pomegranate in the U.S., as well as by a number of European companies.

The greatest conflict of the decade was over whether the U.S. should be involved in a war in Vietnam. It wasn't just "hawks" vs. "doves"; there were also veterans and veterans' moms against the war, conscientious objectors, and others.

Again, there is not much contemporary postcard documentation of the social conflict in the U.S. over Vietnam, but more recently published postcards are beginning to cover this subject. There are a good number of viewcards of Vietnam as it appeared in the 1960s: views of the cities, countryside, and of U.S. military presence. An example from a series of real photo cards of unknown quantity is illustrated on the following page; the title is in French and English on the front and the Vietnamese photographer is named on the back.

A more common series of views of Vietnam are the chromes published by Asia-Pacific Color Productions Ltd. of Hong Kong and printed by Mike Roberts of California. The titles are in English, and they were certainly produced for consumption by American military service personnel. The stock numbers I have seen are in the SC9000, SC10000, and SC11000 sequences. M.G. Price of Ann Arbor, an active collector and trader of foreign view cards, estimates that there

Political cartoon (reproduced on a postcard by Mothers of Servicemen, South Pasadena, CA, courtesy of *The Tidings*, Los Angeles, October 7, 1966) highlights contradictions of the Cold War.

Black and white real photo postcard of a Vietnamese peasant girl. Mailed November 5, 1965, with U.S. Navy free franking from Bud to a captain at the U.S. Naval Hospital in Oakland, CA, it reads, "Things seem to be fairly quiet right now—not much rain—lots of sunshine. Hope things are going along well for you."

are less than 100 different views in this series. Mike Fairley of Seattle, an avid collector of Vietnam views from all decades, estimates that half of his collection of cards of this series are unused and that most of the rest went through military mail and were given free franking. It's important to note that even this so-called "common" series is not easy to find. Searching dealers' stocks at postcard shows, one discovers that very few even have a "Vietnam" category.

The majority of postcards from this 1963 to 1972 decade have little to do with conflict. What they have in common is their "sameness" or "uniformity." The postcards of one city's main street, airport, ballpark, courthouse, national bank, or Methodist church look much like the postcards of another city. This uniformity of tone and style was a result of the relatively few companies that manufactured postcards.

The expanding interstate highway system also had an impact on the trend toward uniformity. Downtown shopping districts were replaced by suburban malls with identical Sears, Wards, and Radio Shacks. "Mom and pop" motels and restaurants found along U.S. highways boasted one-of-a-kind names, styles, and services. They were replaced by chain motels

Top right: Advertising postcard printed by Curt Teich for the Holiday Inn in Vincennes, IN. Note the period hairdos. Mailed September 18, 1965, but the card's 3DK prefix indicates that it was first produced in 1963 (the K represents the print style: a color card with chrome finish). Bottom right: Early-'60s McDonald's postcard. Note "Speedy" character (who preceded Ronald McDonald) under the arch. Mailed with a bulk permit out of Chicago for the Higgins Road, Elk Grove, IL, location, it promotes McDonald's new "Wisconsin aged Cheddar cheese creation," i.e. cheeseburgers.

and restaurants at bypass exits where a key selling point was their uniform recognizability from one city to the next. (An extreme example of this is that in 1993 I can stay at Motel 6's all over the country which have identical room layouts and identical bedspreads!) Wacky roadside attractions which encouraged spur-of-the-moment decisions to stop and take a break were replaced by massive "Great America" and Disney-style entertainment parks around which entire weekends and vacations were planned. The advertising postcards of this decade are a fruitful hunting ground for the last of "mom and pop" individualism and the beginning of entirely new collecting topics such as Holiday Inns, McDonald's, and other chains.

This decade was an exciting one for automotive postcards. According to car enthusiast Bill Hanson, a postcard dealer from Ben Lomond, California, postcards of the '63 Corvette hardtop with split rear window are especially desirable. Other stars of the '60s are the '65 Mustang, which marked the introduction of small sporty-type "pony" cars; and the '65 Pontiac GTO, the first of the "muscle" cars. Manufacturers' advertising cards, both postally-used and unused, are more desirable than museum-produced postcards. In the racing field, cards of Jim Clark, influential in drivers' converting to rear-engine cars, demand special interest.

Dated event postcards from this decade include presidential elections: Johnson-Humphrey vs. Goldwater-Miller (1964); Nixon-Agnew vs.

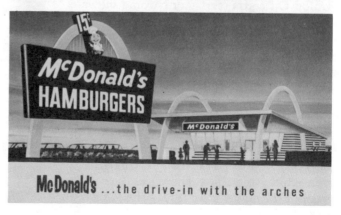

Humphrey-Muskie (1968); and Nixon-Agnew vs. McGovern-(Eagleton replaced by) Shriver (1972). American Party candidate George Wallace and running mate Curtis LeMay added interest to the 1968 election. All of these candidates appear on postcards. An extremely common campaign card of this period is a 1972 view of the Nixon family at the piano. A group of "coattail" campaign cards for 1964 show Senatorial and Representative candidates with the popular President Johnson. Political collector Hal Ottaway of Wichita, Kansas, believes this is the largest group of coattail postcards, with over 20 different examples known.

World's Fairs include New York World's Fair (1964-65); Expo 67 (Montreal); and Japan World Exposition (Osaka, Expo '70). Olympic events include Innsbruck and Tokyo (1964); Mexico City (1968); and Sapporo, Japan, and Munich (1972). All of these events are desirable subjects for a collection of postcards from this decade.

Other subjects to look for: scientific/technical advances—heart transplants and walks on the moon. Also, sporting events: Super Bowl, pennant race, boxing, tennis, and horse racing postcards.

Of the entertainers, Marilyn Monroe and Elvis Presley were icons for the masses, while the Beatles caused mass-hysteria. Their postcards, produced during, before, and since this decade, are all collectible; values generally are highest for the oldest.

The most exciting postcards of the decade were produced to advertise Bill Graham's rock concerts at the Fillmore Auditorium, Fillmore West,

Top: 1963 Chevrolet Corvette Sting Ray Sport Coupe. Note the split-back rear window, which was featured for only one year. Center: A 3-on-1 multiview of the New York World's Fair, 1964-1965, shows the Fountain of Planets at night, the Unisphere, and Shea Stadium. This "official" world's fair postcard, printed by Dexter Press, has both a Dexter stock number (those I've seen are in the 88000-B and 89000-B sequences) and a "WF-" number (this one is WF-90). Many exhibitors' "unofficial" postcards were also printed by Dexter Press. Bottom: Postcard promoting Morris Katz's "instant art" reproductions laminated onto plaques. The backside also offers his 36-card U.S. Presidents set for $5.00. Card number 95793-C, printed by Dexter Press.

Over-size postcard (4-5/8"x7") advertising the July 9-14, 1968, Bill Graham concert, "Blues Bash," at the Fillmore Auditorium in San Francisco, CA. Featured music was by Electric Flag, Blue Cheer, Buddy Guy, Ike & Tina Turner, and Freddy King, and lights by Holy See. Card number BG-127, illustrated by Lee Conklin; printed by Tea Lautrec Litho, San Francisco.

Winterland, and Avalon Ballrooms in San Francisco. Many of these artist-drawn creations show a turn-of-the-century art nouveau influence. The majority are highly imaginative. Sizes vary (approximately 5"x 7"). The brilliantly-colored designs also appeared on posters and concert tickets. The earliest issues first appeared as handbills with blank backs and only later were reprinted with postcard backs.

The Family Dog series (numbers FD-1 through FD-147) advertised concerts from February 1966 through November 1968. The Bill Graham postcards (numbers BG-1 through BG-287) advertised concerts in 1966 through 1971. Many of these postcards are rare, but even more difficult to find are postcards for rock concerts in Denver, Detroit, at the Fillmore East, and at other eastern venues. The period and the art are well documented, and the designs illustrated in Paul Grushkin's monograph *The Art of Rock: Posters from Presley to Punk* (Abbeville Press, 1987). Among the artists contributing to these series were Lee Conklin, Rick Griffin, Greg Irons, Alton Kelley, Bonnie MacLean, Victor Moscoso, Stanley Mouse, David Singer, Randy Tuten, and Wes Wilson.

Other notable artists whose work appeared on '60s-era postcards are Morris Katz: a long sequence of Judaica and a U.S. Presidents set; and Walter and Margaret Keane: illustrations of people with very large dark eyes.

Greeting cards, one of the mainstays of antique postcards, are strikingly absent in this decade. Then, as now, Hallmark or other publishers may have pro-duced a few postcard greetings each year, but I have seen none.

The '60s is my nostalgic decade. These are some of the key events and postcards of the period. I hope you enjoy searching for and collecting them!

✳

Diane Allmen is founding editor of *Postcard Collector* magazine (1983-1988, Krause Publications, Iola, WI) and author of *The Official Identification and Price Guide to Postcards* (1990, House of Collectibles, New York). With partner Dave Long, she co-owns Modern Postcard Sales of Elkhart, Indiana, specialists in chromes and current-issue postcards. She collects Vinegar Valentines; Century of Progress; Women's Suffrage; views of Chicago and places of personal interest; as well as Chromes and Moderns.

AMERICA WAKES UP TO REALITY

By Susan Brown Nicholson

The threat of a nuclear disaster was just one reality Americans faced in the mid-1970s. "What's all this nonsense..." © Terry Davis, One World Artist Cooperative, New Haven, CT, supports the development of renewable energy sources and says no to nuclear power and arms.

✴

Many collectors don't see any reason to collect cards from this time period. Wake up! Many of the rare and unusual cards from the Golden Age commanding the highest prices relate to the social and political history of that time. The cards I have featured from 1973 to 1982 also deal with the social and political history of the period, and will truly be the collected cards from that decade.

To best describe 1973 to 1982, I would say it is when America woke up to reality. We, as a people, realized we were not going to win every war, and some we should not even be fighting. We finally got out of Vietnam.

It was a time of greater understanding and tolerance of the many diverse cultures and lifestyles in this country. Gay Rights, Pro Choice, ERA, Apartheid, Cocaine, Antismoking: all became a part of our vocabulary.

It was a time of celebration; America had its 200th birthday—the Bicentennial. Then, just five years later, 750 million people worldwide watched Charles and Di get married.

It was a time of sadness when John Lennon, Mao Tsetung, Golda Meir, and Richard Daley died; Mount Saint Helens erupted; America pulled out of the Olympics; and President Nixon was forced to resign.

Americans were forced to become aware of the world's limited resources as a nationwide fuel shortage hit, causing several states to ra-

tion gasoline. We became more aware of another precious resource, our health. More people quit smoking or never started. We joined a renewed physical fitness regime with a glut of new exercise equipment, workout videos, and diet-health clubs.

By the end of the decade capitalism reigned, and the Yuppies were winning. By 1973, inflation had risen to 8.8 percent, the largest increase in any year since 1947. The stock market soared, junk bonds became king, and the ride wasn't over until Black Monday in October of 1987.

This period, 1973-1982, saw many changes, both good and bad. In the '70s, more women went to college and held a wider variety of jobs than ever before, with 40 percent of American women being college graduates.

In 1972, the Senate approved the House bill of 1971 calling for a women's Equal Rights Amendment (ERA). By the middle of 1975, 34 states had ratified the amendment, but it needed 38 to be passed. It was

Advertising card for Korns Korner Postcards supports the Equal Rights Ammendment. © Helaine Victoria Press.

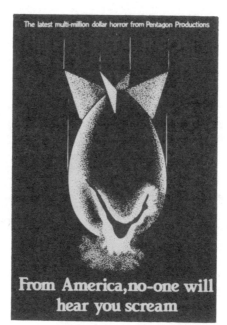

The latest multi-million dollar horror from Pentagon Productions

From America, no-one will hear you scream

Cocaine

Postcards reflecting the reality of the times. Clockwise from top left: "Nancy's Lawn Sale" by Coral-Lee. Anti-bomb message from England's Leeds Postcards. "Cocaine" by Americard. Who could have guessed what would follow for these two? British card by Photo Precision Limited. "Bi-Heeled," © The American Postcard Company, New York City, presents a subtle gay rights message. The London-based British Union for the Abolition of Vivisection fights against all animal experiments, including for medical research. Raquel's *Total Beauty and Fitness* video demonstrates how she stays "completely in shape."

The Marriage of The Prince of Wales

and

Lady Diana Spencer
29 July 1981

THORN EMI VIDEO

"It's my way to stay completely in shape."
— RAQUEL WELCH

RAQUEL

TOTAL BEAUTY AND FITNESS

AGAINST ALL ANIMAL EXPERIMENTS

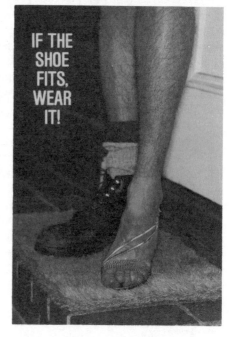

IF THE SHOE FITS, WEAR IT!

defeated. Postcards were made for each side of the issue.

In the early '70s, most states prohibited abortions. Then, in 1973, the Supreme Court ruled that the states could not forbid a woman to have an abortion. (Roe vs. Wade) Nearly 20 years later this pro-choice issue is still being debated. Postcards from the '70s were plain and to the point, "I'm Pro-Choice...and I VOTE!"

Mutual fund IRAs were the retirement investment of choice for many of the '70s Yuppies. Advertising card from an investment manager at Wayne Hummer & Co., Chicago

The focus was on politics in 1973. Vietnam ended; Nixon discontinued the draft; the Watergate scandal erupted; Agnew resigned because of investigation of graft; and in late October impeachment hearings concerning President Nixon began before the House Judiciary Committee.

Then on August 9, 1974, Richard Nixon resigned under fire of certain impeachment. On September 8, President Gerald Ford granted Nixon a full pardon on all federal crimes. Ford said it was to "reconcile divisions in our country and heal the wounds that had festered too long."

Presidential campaigning dominated 1975 with Jimmy Carter being elected. And, all citizens were abuzz with plans for the nation's Bicentennial. The United States celebrated its 200th birthday with festivities throughout the land. One postcard I have is of a large billboard, erected in a small town in Iowa, that reads, "Two hundred years ago on this site absolutely nothing happened." This card was designed by the letter-writing humorist (L.L.) Lowell Loper. It is one of my favorites.

All of 1976 saw a renewed interest in America and patriotism. This was the year I became involved with postcards. I did my first postcard show ever in Saint Louis. The hot topic then was, you guessed it, the Fourth of July and all patriotic

"Spirit of '76" theme is taken from a 1915 postcard by Rose O'Neill and adapted by artist Florence Baker.

postcards. Prices for these cards have never been as high as that year. Many non-collectors just wanted something patriotic, whatever the price. I started my antique and modern postcard collection that year. I have always collected items by Rose O'Neill, and the modern Bicentennial postcards I acquired were more to add to that collection than the postcard collection. As I taught myself about the Golden Age cards, I applied the same principles to contemporary cards, thus the illustrations here.

In 1976, Russia, the United States, and 13 other countries began top-secret talks in London to curb the spread of nuclear weapons. The English postcards concerning this subject are great and can fill an entire album with meaningful, cleverly designed cards. Yet, on a grassroots level without bombs, without weapons, black school children took to the streets of South Africa to reject apartheid that year. This national uprising resulted in hundreds being shot and thousands detained or exiled. The International Defence and Aid Fund produced an eight-card set titled "Children in Apartheid South Africa." Watch for other cards.

Cover from an eight-card set, "Children in Apartheid South Africa," produced by the International Defence and Aid Fund for Southern Africa.

America and Russia renewed their space programs in 1977 with the Russians setting "days in space" records and the U.S. launching the space shuttle *Enterprise*. Our fascination with space is recorded on many postcards.

The energy crisis of 1977 saw long gasoline lines and a blackout that paralyzed New York City and Westchester County for 25 hours. As energy became foremost on the minds of the public, 1978 saw heating bills soar as blizzards covered 1000 miles from the Midwest to the East Coast, dumping up to 31 inches of snow in 24 hours. This natural energy-eating weather system did not let up, and again in 1979 blizzards struck the Midwest, killing over 100 people. The national 55 mph speed limit, designed to curb energy use, was the subject of postcards.

In 1978, jumps were made in science with

FLORIDA 55 MPH

Give a darn... Save Gas. Life

FLORIDA ARRIVE ALIVE SUNSHINE STATE

GOVERNOR'S HIGHWAY SAFETY COMMISSION

Florida Department of Administration

The Governor's Highway Safety Commission from the Florida Department of Administration used postcards to promote their 55 mph safety campaign designed to combat highway accidents and save gas.

the first baby conceived outside of a woman's body being born in England and our vocabulary was extended to include "Test Tube Baby."

On one coast, in 1978, money was being thrown away as the first legal gambling casinos opened in Atlantic City, and on the other coast, California taxpayers screamed, "Enough is enough!" voting in Proposition 13, which cut property taxes by 57 percent. Postcards, yes.

Whether the gambling or taxes had anything to do with it, the "Grey Panthers," as the senior citizen activists were known, demanded and got the mandatory U.S. retirement age raised from 65 to 70 that year.

Later in 1978, Congress deregulated the airline industry resulting in air travel becoming more affordable to more people than ever before. Yet, three courageous Americans decided to bypass the commercial air system and completed the first transatlantic balloon crossing. Are there postcards?

In January of 1979 the surgeon general's 1200-page report sited overwhelming evidence linking smoking to cancer, heart and lung diseases, and other illnesses. I have collected antismoking postcards and early cards featuring smoking, even one with a fish smoking.

Then on March 28, 1979, the accident at Three Mile Island nuclear reactor in Pennsylvania occurred, arousing fears of major loss of life. On May 6, 1979, 65,000

persons demonstrated against nuclear power in Washington, D.C. On May 18, a jury awarded $10.5 million in damages to the estate of Karen Silkwood, a lab technician contaminated by radiation while working at a Kerr-McGee plutonium plant. Later, Silkwood's story was told by Hollywood, and postcards were issued.

The Ayatollah Khomeini returned to Iran in 1979, after 15 years in exile. As the decade rolled over to the '80s, the Shah of Iran died

The London-based organization, War on Want, wages a campaign against world poverty through an anti-smoking campaign. Published by Leeds Postcards.

in a military hospital in Egypt; gold soared to $835 per ounce up from $311 just

Two reasons why we should question tobacco production in the Third World.

days before; and so many countries became frustrated with Russia's invasion of Afghanistan that they withdrew from the 1980 Moscow Olympics.

I was in Europe when the final decision came that America would not be participating in the Olympics. I got in a car and drove to the first available Communist country to try to buy postcards of the event. I found no cards, but purchased many Olympic posters from that year, including two the Communist border guard cut off the wall for me. I celebrated my birthday by sleeping on the floor of a

Left: A New York City Times Square marquee notes the passing of a music legend. © The American Postcard Co. Right: Before and after the Mount St. Helens eruption. © Mike Roberts Color Productions.

JOHN LENNON 1940-1980

MOUNT ST HELENS BEFORE AND AFTER

Czechoslovakia taxi cab driver's house when I could not find a hotel that would open its doors in Prague at midnight. What a person won't do to find a postcard.

Many sad events occurred in 1980, John Lennon was gunned down in New York, and Mount St. Helens erupted killing at least 31 persons and hurling steam and ash 60,000 feet into the sky. Hot rock and gas flattened trees in a 120-square-mile area. I purchased postcards that were issued for these events, but it was not until I visited Mount St. Helens this last year did I get a true feel of the devastation. It is the closest thing I will ever experience to being on the moon, and this is a decade later. The biggest tragedy of that year was the fire that raged through the MGM Grand Hotel in Las Vegas killing 84 persons.

In 1980, the military made the news with the graduation of the first woman from a U.S. military academy and the announcement of the "Stealth" aircraft that can evade radar detection. Many postcards are available of this new flying machine.

Yet, the '80s had a sense of humor about it. We watched Billy Carter embarrass his President brother by registering as an agent of the Libyan government and issuing his own brand of beer. The whole political arena of Jimmy and Billy reminded me of something I read when researching Roosevelt. The reporters were questioning him about his daughter, Alice, and her antics. They saw her on the roof of the White House smoking. What did he think of that?

He replied, "I can either run the country or I can watch Alice, but I can't do both!"

So, Jimmy was thrown out of office and we, not loosing our sense of humor, replaced him with a

"Watt is a Great American," © Sandra Willard, One World Artist Cooperative, makes a satirical statement about the ideas of the former Secretary of the Interior.

movie star. The Reagan era began and the satirical postcards are abundant, mainly because of the publisher Coral-Lee. Nancy taught us to "Just say No," and their son danced in his underwear on television. Many comical cards were issued during this administration.

On the serious side, James Watt, Secretary of the Interior, came under fire during this administration mainly because of his ridiculous ideas about the environment—and postcards were made.

Central America became a hotbed of activity in the '80s. Archbishop Romero was assassinated while celebrating mass. He had been quoted as saying, "Me they can kill but the clamor for justice among the people, they cannot silence." Postcards were issued for "Solidarity with El Salvador's People." The message side of the cards reads, "Stop Yankee Imperialism in Central America."

On Hiroshima Day in 1981, the United States announced its decision to produce the neutron bomb! The neutron bomb leaves property intact, relying upon massive radiation to kill all living things. This outraged the European states, which had already rejected this bomb, resulting in a barrage of postcards.

While this may seem more like a history lesson than a postcard lesson, it is to remind you of events which were part of the social and political history of that ten years. Postcards were issued to record each of these events. Did you save yours or throw them away? This record could go on and on. Postcards recorded the "punk" generation of clothing and hair styles, the starvation in the world, the extended use of cocaine by every cross section of America. The fight to stop the use of animals in laboratories or killing them for fashion is all recorded on cards.

B-2 Stealth Bomber. Photo © H. Dexter Garey. Distributed by Smith-Western Co.

When I hear collectors complain, "I can't afford to collect cards anymore," I want to scream...why not, some of the best is free!!! Take a look at the cards available from these last few decades that still are well within the reach of every budget. Don't give up the fun, just shift gears.

✳

Susan Brown Nicholson, noted postcard dealer and collector, is a regular columnist for *Postcard Collector* in addition to having authored numerous other collectible articles and books, among which is *The Antique Postcards of Rose O'Neill*, written in conjunction with Janet A. Banneck.

Yesterday Today & Tomorrow

By Dave Long

Disasters depicted on modern cards are as difficult to find as they are popular with collectors. Here, Hurricane Hugo, which struck Charleston, SC, on September 21-22, 1989, is documented on a computer-enhanced satellite photo. Card #364-E © Charleston Post Card Co., Inc. Photo by NOAA.

✳

The past ten are my favorite postcard years. It was in mid-1983 that I formed a small postcard service, offering current issues of modern chromes to collectors nationwide. That service continues today, and with it the wealth of knowledge gained through countless contacts made with distributors and printers. Many exciting things happened during this decade; some dramatic, others more subtle. All have worked together, to one degree or another, to produce a postcard product and marketplace that is more diversified and appealing than ever in its long and rich history. And now, let's take a look at some of the things which helped to shape these past ten years.

With few exceptions (notably flat-finished, wooden, metallic, 3-D, and other novelty types), the primary postcard offered during this period was the glossy-finished chrome. By 1983, the standard size 3-1/2"x 5-1/2" card could still be found, as it can today in some areas of the country, but in very limited numbers. In its place, the more common 4"x6" continental continued to expand its share of the marketplace. This changeover was gradual, but steady. Coincidentally, another and even larger postcard was making

This full-bleed card from the '80s offers a design twist with its 4/1 multiview of the visit of Pope John Paul II to Detroit in 1987. From Perrin Souvenir Distributors; photos and design by Jersy Jander.

steady inroads into the marketplace, especially in select large cities and high-traffic tourist areas. Collectors have generally not found these 4-1/2"x6-1/2" and 5"x7" cards very appealing because of difficulty in storage/filing and price. Tourists, on the other hand, have helped them to become a substantial part of the overall market in such places as Boston, Chicago, New York City, St. Louis, New Orleans, California, Florida, and elsewhere.

In 1983, the king of style dictated a black-bordered card. It was seen as sleek, sophisticated, and very desirable. Since then, state-of-the-art style has produced a rainbow offering of colored borders, key-lines,

stylized lettering, a variety of colored graphics and, in the past few years, even a return to the full-bleed card with absolutely nothing but the picture or design. Today's leading viewcard distributors typically offer a variety of styles. Those who distribute other than viewcards typically offer full-bleed or narrow white-bordered cards.

By the early 1980s, such dominant chrome printers as Curt Teich, Dexter Press, Koppel, Plastichrome, and others were either on their way out or completely gone. Since then, the founder of Mike Roberts Color Productions has passed away, and the once-popular name of H.S. Crocker is no more. In their places we still see the Mike Roberts name, but to a lesser degree than in the past and from a reorganized firm, and Curt Teich through its new owner under the name John Hinde Curteich Inc. John Hinde also produces cards under the name Plastichrome.

Other current domestic printers include Lawson-Mardon, Color Press, McGrew Color Graphics, and International Color Systems. Many smaller firms also exist, and several distributors even own their own printing equipment or firms. All appear to have expanded their business during the past decade, but the fact remains that a very large portion of the postcards sold in this country are produced outside our shores. Whether this is an expanding, stable, or declining trend is difficult to ascertain. Time will tell. There does seem, however, to be an increased demand for "Made in the USA," and it wouldn't surprise me to see this have a positive impact on domestic postcard production in the years to come.

T he scope of subjects covered during the past ten years was pretty exceptional all around the country with respect to views. Everything worth photographing was! A major gap, however, seems to be the documentation of "people" activities, changes in progress, special and annual events, disasters, civil disorder, sporting events, contests and pageants, political events, armed forces activities, and the like. There just wasn't very much done with any of these subjects, and likely there won't be in the years to come. At least not by viewcard distributors! In general, postcard quality continued to improve during the past decade, as has point-of-purchase appeal. By comparison to 1983 postcards, those issued in 1992 seemed brighter and fresher. They offered considerable new photography (in contrast to the common practice of reprinting older views and enhancing them with new borders or graphics), were printed on a better quality of paper, enjoyed a better coating or lamination, and appeared to have used an improved color separation process. All this, when combined with the graphics variation of 1992 cards, made them more attractive than ten years before.

"The National Bean," published by American Postcard Co., Inc., New York, takes a satirical look at President Reagan's obsession with jelly beans. Photograph © Alfred Gescheidt.

It isn't possible to completely cover all of the noteworthy and collectible postcards issued during the past ten years, but some which come to mind and will be treasured in the years to come are described in the following paragraphs.

The political scene is a popular collectible subject. The most prolific publisher of political postcards ceased operation in 1985 with the issuance of standard-size views of President Reagan's second term inauguration ceremonies in January. The publisher...Coral-Lee, of course. She produced hundreds of standard-size cards of political interest beginning with President Carter's term in office. Other cards produced in the 1980s include those offered at the Reagan Library in Simi Valley, California, an array of humorous offerings of Reagan and Bush (and their wives) by American Postcard Company, political satire by Matt Wuerker (Preziosi Postcards), Liz Wensjoe (Great Ideas of Miami), and others, plus the typical range of viewcards depicting presidential portraits, their wives, and their homes.

We experienced two major events in 1984, the Los Angeles Summer Games and the Louisiana World Exposition. Each provided a large group of both official and unofficial views. The same is true for the 10th Pan American Games, held in Indianapolis in 1987. Although they were Canadian events, the impact of a vast array of official and unofficial views from Expo 86, held in Vancouver, and the Calgary 1988 Winter Olympic Games

The Louisiana World Exposition, held in New Orleans May 12-November 11, 1984, provided for a wealth of official views, such as this one, #B14110.

✳ 53

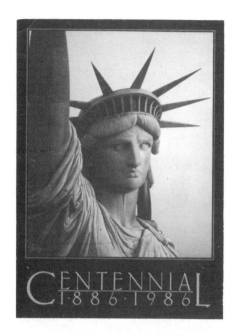

was vigorously followed here in the States.

The 1986 Statue of Liberty centennial celebration was well documented and included a wonderful assortment by Impact. Perrin Souvenir Distributors issued a commemorative 4/1 multiview of the September 19, 1987, visit of Pope John Paul II to Hamtramck, Michigan. Michigan celebrated its sesquicentennial that year, as documented by three Penrod/Hiawatha commemoratives. Several views were issued by White House Publishing Co. in conjunction with Cincinnati's 1988 bicentennial celebration. 1989 and 1990 saw several western states celebrate their centennials—Washington, Idaho, Montana, Wyoming, North and South Dakota. Cards were issued in limited numbers for each of these celebrations. Sequoia and Yosemite National Parks saw centennial commemoratives issued in 1990 by Scope Enterprises. Several distributors issued special cards for the 50th anniversary of Mount Rushmore in 1991. In 1992, a commemorative was issued by Molloy for Kentucky's bicentennial celebration and at least 12 cards were published in preparation for the Oregon Trail's 150th anniversary in 1993, most by Smith-Western.

A variety of cards appeared during 1991 in conjunction with Operation Desert Storm, including troop support, patriotics,

and President Bush tossing tie clips to the troops. Numerous views were issued by Molloy and Victory Postcards in conjunction with the 500th anniversary of Columbus' discovery of America. An attractive embossed standard size card was issued that same year for the World Columbian Stamp Expo '92, held May 22-31 in Chicago. Not to be overlooked, Route 66 celebrated its 66th birthday in 1992, as noted on a commemorative issued by the Missouri Postcard Co.

Disasters are as hard to find on modern cards as they are popular with collectors. I recall four cards that were issued of Hurricane Hugo, which struck Charleston, South Carolina, on September 21-22, 1989; several of the October 17, 1989, San Francisco earthquake; two of the March 13, 1990, tornado that ravished Sumner County, Kansas; and a single view of the Lake Washington Floating Bridge, which sank during a storm on November 25, 1990. Such views are very collectible.

Sporting events made their presence felt on many cards issued during the past decade; in particular, those published for the various Super Bowls. Other dated sports events include the Indy 500 and other auto races, the Kentucky Derby, and miscellaneous marathons held around the country. One card even pictures a close-up of the official pace car for the May 26, 1991, Coca-Cola 600, held at the Charlotte Motor Speedway.

The past ten years also saw the production of many other great cards, including those issued for postcard clubs, postcard shows, and National Post Card Week, which is celebrated each May. Some feature home-drawn art or themes, while others are professionally done and offer the art of well-known postcard artists such as Ann Rusnak and Rick Geary. A cute artist-drawn series was published over a several-year period during the 1980s by Dunlap Post Card Co., and features the work of David Luebke.

Cause cards were issued for AIDS, Gay Rights, Endangered Species, Save The Bay, and Women's Rights. Beautiful reproduc-

Many sites across America celebrated a "coming of age" during this decade. Among those birthdays captured on postcards were (left to right): 100th—Sequoia National Park, © Scope Enterprises, Clovis, CA. 50th—Mount Rushmore, © Western Souvenirs, Inc., Rapid City, SD. 100th—Washington, published by Outdoor Photo, Olympia, WA. 150th—The Oregon Trail, published by Smith-Western, Inc., Portland, OR. 150th—Michigan, © Penrod/Hiawatha Co., Berrien Center, MI. 100th—North Dakota, distributed by Saks News, Inc., Bismarck, ND. 200th—Cincinnati, © White House Publishing Co. Inc., Cincinnati, OH.

Postcards were readily used in the '80s and early '90s to announce postcard events. John H. McClintock published this example for the 15th annual King of Prussia Sale & Show (near right). Reproductions were also popular. Shown at far right is an early Coca-Cola design produced in postcard form by the company itself.

tions were published throughout the period of early Coca-Cola designs, crate label art, illustrations for auto advertisements, World War I & II posters, and old Civil War photos. Still other exciting lines included stills from several Disney movies ("Fantasia," "Jungle Book," and "The Little Mermaid"), "Star Trek" and "Star Wars," "Saturday Night Live," "Dracula," "The Addams Family," a new series of Marilyn Monroe, the photography of Annie Leibovitz, Marvel Comics covers, and on and on.

During this same period was the production of wonderful cards depicting our major cities and towns, and their continually changing skylines. There undoubtedly are as many good cards and series from this period not covered as those which were, but suffice it to say that the years 1983-1992 were productive indeed, and filled with a volume of good, collectible material.

What lies in the future for our domestic postcard market? I wish I had a crystal ball, for then I'd know. However, since that isn't possible, I can only make some guesses. It seems logical that the continental card will continue to be the mainstay of the industry, but that the market share of oversize views will grow steadily in the larger marketplaces. Styles and quality should continue to change and improve as new ideas, techniques, and equipment enter the picture. I feel that competition will dictate these changes as well as a continued improvement in the general quality of photography.

I forecast little change in domestic versus foreign printing, at least for the next few years and until such time as more domestic firms begin using state-of-the-art equipment, consider view postcard printing to be their primary endeavor, and place a higher importance on the value of customer service.

An educated guess suggests that non-views will capture a larger share of the market in the years to come. I'm certain the viewcard side of the industry will continue to grow at a healthy rate, but that the non-viewcard publishers will grow at a

more rapid rate, including firms such as Classico San Francisco, Art Unlimited, Pomegranate, Fotofolio, American Postcard Co., and others.

I feel the scope of coverage will remain about the same as it has in the past, but if we are to see an increase in documentation, it will have to come from other than our current postcard publishers and/or distributors. Private individuals and concerns may well have to take up the slack. Time will tell!

✳

Route or Trail—both of these byways led to adventure. Left: Route 66, 2200 miles of highway connecting Chicago with Los Angeles, marked its 66th anniversary in 1992. The Missouri Postcard Co. commemorates the event on card #MPC 9201. Right: Intended for use as a trade route to the west, the Santa Fe Trail was established in 1821. It took two months to travel by covered wagon. Art © David Luebke and Dunlap Post Card Co., Omaha.

Dave Long has collected postcards since 1949 and from the very first has specialized in moderns. For the past decade he has sold modern postcards to collectors; since July 1989 with Diane Allmen under the name Modern Postcard Sales. Since the first issue of *Postcard Collector*, he has authored the monthly column "Small Talk," which discusses findings and trends in the field of modern postcards as seen through his eyes.

Home of the Coca-Cola 600, the Charlotte Motor Speedway and its official pace car are captured on this key-line bordered view, published by Aerial Photography Services, Inc., Charlotte, NC.

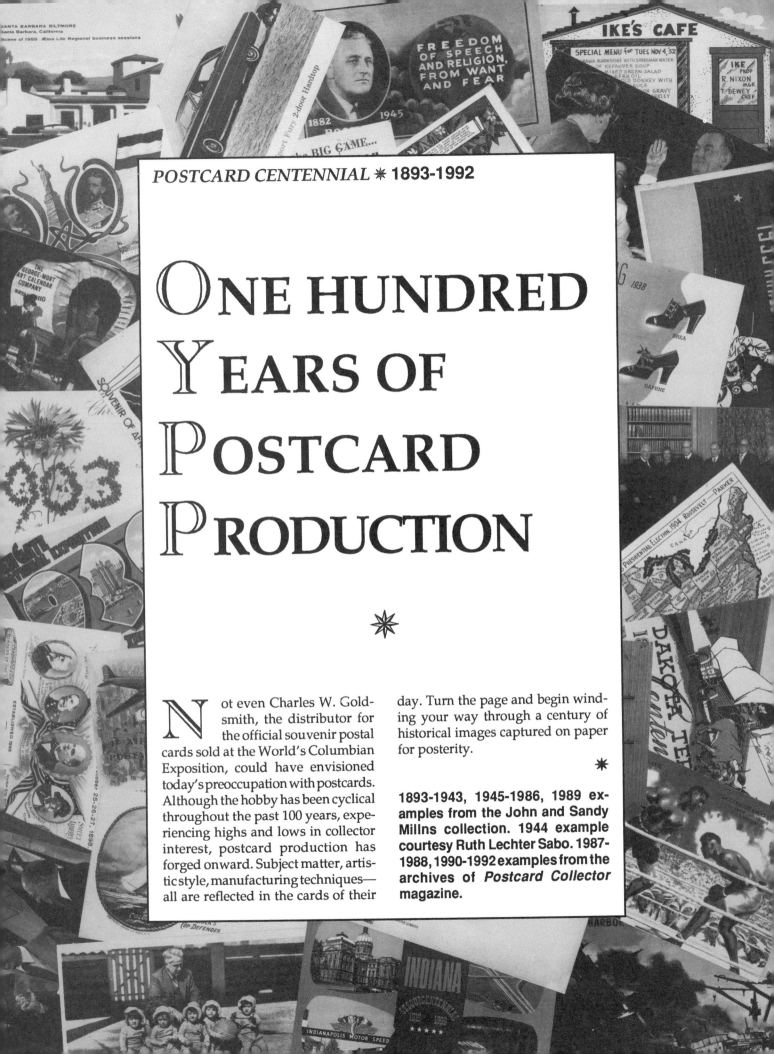

POSTCARD CENTENNIAL ✳ **1893-1992**

ONE HUNDRED YEARS OF POSTCARD PRODUCTION

✳

Not even Charles W. Goldsmith, the distributor for the official souvenir postal cards sold at the World's Columbian Exposition, could have envisioned today's preoccupation with postcards. Although the hobby has been cyclical throughout the past 100 years, experiencing highs and lows in collector interest, postcard production has forged onward. Subject matter, artistic style, manufacturing techniques—all are reflected in the cards of their day. Turn the page and begin winding your way through a century of historical images captured on paper for posterity.

✳

1893-1943, 1945-1986, 1989 examples from the John and Sandy Millns collection. 1944 example courtesy Ruth Lechter Sabo. 1987-1988, 1990-1992 examples from the archives of *Postcard Collector* magazine.

1893: Printed and distributed by *Puck*, well-known Chicago humor magazine, at the World's Columbian Exposition grounds.

1894: Lyle & McCance's advertising postcard promoted their business as well as serving as an order form for distributors.

1895: From a set of 12 Boston area views by the American Souvenir Co., Boston. Printed by Armstrong & Co. Lith., Boston.

1896: German Gruss vom Ocean card by Jacobsen & Peip, Leipzig, detailing the voyage from Bremen to New York City.

1908: Cook claimed that he discovered the North Pole in April 1908. Perry said not. Does this map card answer the question?

1907: Metropolitan News Co. published this card to welcome guests to Boston's Old Home Week, held July 28-August 3.

1906: Pike Centennial Celebration, Colorado Springs, honored the explorer who first sighted the mountain, ©J. Lisle Warren.

1905: A careful look makes the word Dartmouth stand out from this Princeton mascot's stripes. So much for team loyalty!

1909: Wright aeroplane on Governor's Island, New York Harbor, before a flight. Shows canoe carried on trips over water.

1910: A tribute to baseball player Honus Wagner and his hometown Carnegie, Pennsylvania, by the Pittsburgh *Gazette Times*.

1911: Camp #192 of the fraternal organization Woodmen of the World invites members to its annual o'possom [sic] supper.

1912: Utilizing a coast-to-coast aviation advertising campaign, Vin Fiz, "the sparkling grape drink," was the talk of America.

1924: The 8th Summer Olympics were held in Paris in 1924. An artist's rendition of a boxing bout highlights one of the events.

1923: Tommy Milton, winner of the Indianapolis 500, at the wheel of H.C.S. Special. Real photo postcard by W. Frank Jones.

1922: Friends and relatives were invited to attend Mrs. Julian R. Enck's funeral and interment via this postcard message.

1921: In the first match to draw a "million-dollar gate," Dempsey retained his heavyweight title against Georges Carpentier.

1925: Ku Klux Klan members openly gather for the Labor Day festivities in Pontiac, Michigan, on this 1925 real photo card.

1926: Baseball great Rogers Hornsby joins fellow St. Louis Cardinals in honor of their winning the National League pennant.

1927: The folk tale "pigs root ahead while fowl scratch backwards" may be the reason pigs are common on New Year cards.

1928: Milwaukee, Wisconsin, residents welcomed the German-Irish Bremen Flyers to their city and county on May 13-14.

1897: James Corbett lost his world heavyweight boxing title to Bob Fitzsimmons in a March 17 fight at Carson City, Nevada.

1898: Event, advertising, patriotic: it's all here on a card published by Arthur Livingston during the Spanish-American War.

1899: In the oldest international sailing race, the yacht *Columbia* defends the America's Cup title on an H.A. Rost, N.Y., card.

1900: Located 40 miles west-northwest of Augusta on Maine's Androscoggin River, Rumford is noted for its paper industry.

1904: A state-by-state breakdown shows Roosevelt soundly defeating Alton B. Parker for President, ©P.C. Kullman & Co.

1903: Raphael Tuck & Sons' "Christmas" postcard series #1806 year date issue also expresses good wishes for the New Year.

1902: E. Buttner & Co. card commemorating Prince Heinrich of Prussia's arrival in New York City to christen the royal yacht.

1901: G.S. Cowper postcard shows McKinley's visit to Goat Island just prior to his fatal shooting at the Pan-American Expo.

1913: The Pacific Coast Casualty Insurance Co. used postcards as a means of sending registration cards to their customers.

1914: According to this advertising card, an additional $175 gained the buyer of an Oldsmobile Six extra seating for three.

1915: A happy crowd is on hand as the last spike is driven at the Chicago Speedway on this Commercial Colortype Co. card.

1916: Commemorating 100 years of gun manufacture by E. Remington & Sons, whos first gun was made in Ilion, New York.

1920: Real photo of John Bistline's first prize sheep flock at the Mercer County Fair (IL? KY? MO? NJ? ND? OH? PA? WV?).

1919: The rise of Jack Dempsey to world heavyweight boxing champion when he knocks out Jess Willard to win the title.

1918: Flag motifs representing World War I allies lend hope for a happy new year on this silk embroidered year date postcard.

1917: St. Paul, Minnesota, combines an announcement for the National Ski Tournament as part of its outdoor sports carnival.

1929: Mexican star Dolores Del Rio was chosen as the film patroness of the 19th National Orange Show in San Bernardino.

1930: Advertisers have been using gimmicks for decades to prove a point, as in this GE sealed-in-steel refrigerator drowning.

1931: H.A. Frahm & Son, Peotone, Illinois, announced via postcard their June new customer sale of Allen-A ladies hosiery.

1932: Geo. W. Burnett of George-Mort Art Calendar Company used advertising cards to announce his impending arrival.

1965: Selling domestic cars took ingenuity in the '60s due to increased foreign imports. Just what is this couple looking for?

1966: 150-year-old Indiana is noted for its Northern Indiana Toll Road, motor speedway, and the nation's largest steel mills.

1967: "The Last of the Torrey Canyon - 28th March, 1967." This real photo offers a significant lack of any other information.

1968: In retrospect, it's unfortunate that Humphrey did not get a turn. Nixon could expect many "limelight days" in his term.

1964: The price per pound of this grand champion steer from the Houston Livestock Show averages out to about $20.50.

1963: One of the most memorable inaugurations is relived on a Southwestern Historical Wax Museum card by Dexter Press.

1962: Ringo Starr hadn't yet replaced drummer Pete Best on this Editions Nugeron card. That event took place later in 1962.

1961: Dakota Territory not only included the present states of North and South Dakota, but much of Montana and Wyoming.

1949: The cost of air mail postal cards increased to four cents on January 10, as is shown on this first-day-of-issue example.

1950: Is this where all of the televangelist pleas for donations began? The message is the same; only the amount has changed.

1951: Winners from 1950 grace this Academy of Motion Picture Arts & Sciences card announcing the 23rd annual ceremony.

1952: Not instantly recognizable as a political card, "Ike's Cafe" makes fun of the Democrats in the November 4th election.

1948: Commemorating the first Woman's Rights Convention centennial is this stamp card featuring reformers of the time.

1947: Disaster hits in this real photo of a ship explosion in Texas City, Texas, harbor that killed 500 and injured another 3000.

1946: The gasoline and tire rationing of the war years is over; new cars are back in vogue, such as this Chevrolet four door.

1945: Roosevelt didn't live to see the end of a war that caused want and fear, dying April 12. Published by Collotype Co.

1933: Art deco and the linen-type process come alive on Chicago World's Fair postcards such as this, ©Arena Co. Chicago.

1934: Two photographs are spliced together to make this real photo of Franklin and Eleanor Roosevelt's visit to Portland.

1935: Harley Davidson lists great advancements in the new models, like cam ground T-slot pistons & prefocused headlights.

1936: The Dionne quintuplets, the first set to live any length of time, celebrate their 2nd year with Dr. Dafoe, ©N.E.A. Inc.

1969: Apollo 11 astronauts make their descent to the moon's surface on this Dixon Lotus Production card from Great Britain.

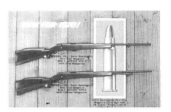

1970: Now 154 years old (see 1916), the Remington Company is still producing new firearms for the outdoor sportsman.

1971: Amberley Greeting Card takes a tongue-in-cheek look at the benefits derived from a "stinking, rotten establishment."

1972: Shortly after the nomination, Eagleton resigned from the ticket, at McGovern's request, due to a history of depression.

1960: Campaigning on the coattails of the national party leaders is a common practice for candidates running for state office.

1959: Aetna Life Insurance used the Santa Barbara Biltmore complex as the site of its regional business meetings in 1959.

1958: No building could accomodate the thousands of faithful Jehovah's Witnesses attending the 1958 New York assembly.

1957: From 6 to 60 horses, Kiekhaefer Mercury had outboard motors with speed capacity for every type of boat or boater.

1953: Refrigerators have come a long way since 1930, as evidenced on this advertising card for Crosley's fine new Shelvador.

1954: Indiana's love of basketball has been noted in books, movies, and even postcards. Milan had the best team this year.

1955: Although unsigned, New Year greetings are offered on what appears to be an original homemade calendar postcard.

1956: Despite this tailor's remark, the Republicans continued to "fit in" for the next four years. Card published by Baxtone.

1944: Passed by U.S. Army Censor #21 and Army Examiner #26322, this card was postmarked April 10 and mailed postage-free.

1943: Allied leaders agree on nothing less than "unconditional surrender" from Axis nations at the Casablanca Conference.

1942: Henry Kramer presents his maraca-wielding Midget Starlets of 1942. Was Dolly Kramer (fourth from right) related?

1941: December 7th attack on Pearl Harbor reproduced from an official Navy photo on a modern postcard by Mike Roberts.

1937: Although January weather makes travel difficult, W.L. Elder hopes for a good turnout at next Saturday's horse sale.

1938: There's not much color to Menihan's spring line of Arch-aid shoes, but what's lacking there is made up for in sturdiness.

1939: Stanley A. Piltz used a large "number" design filled with San Francisco scenes to advertise the Golden Gate Exposition.

1940: Lafayette vs. Lehigh must have been a "big game" if it warranted an advertising card listing Jersey Central's schedule.

1973: On December 3, 1973 *Pioneer X* was the first space probe to fly past Jupiter, coming within 81,000 miles of the planet.

1974: Gerald Ford is sworn in as President at another memorable inauguration, this time due to a scandal in the White House.

1975: Santa is getting a jump on the '76 bicentennial events on this advertising postcard sent to Christmas card distributors.

1976: Clinton, Connecticut, honors 313 years while America celebrates its 200th anniversary on this card by The Color Studio.

1980: America's cold war with the Soviet Union led to a U.S. boycott of the summer Olympics held in Moscow. French card.

1979: Carter is briefed on a Heritage Enterprises card after a breakdown of Three Mile Island's reactor core cooling system.

1978: Discussions between Sadat, Carter, and Begin called for a peace treaty between Egypt and Israel. Card by Coral-Lee.

1977: There are lots of historical moments to be gleaned from this Western Reserve Society postcard announcing their show.

1981: On September 25 Sandra Day O'Connor became the first woman to join the Supreme Court. Postcard by Coral-Lee.

1982: A decade later exploitative beer ads such as this from Pabst Blue Ribbon would come under fire from feminist groups.

1983: Before the centerfold scandal, reigning Miss America Vanessa Williams chats with Ronald Reagan on a Coral-Lee card.

1984: Cold wars had no affect on America's attendance at these games, held on U.S. soil; by Drawing Board Greeting Cards.

1988: *Deltiology has no boundaries* by Andre Roussey—the International Postcard Association honors worldwide collecting.

1987: Sponsored by White Post Restorations, this annual classic car festival is held in White Post, Virginia. I. Lewis painting.

1986: Published by the Stevens Point Area NOW, the founding members of the state organization are honored after 20 years.

1985: The success of the historic relationship between Reagan and Gorbachev began at their first arms summit in Geneva.

1989: Herst u Verlag Schoning & Co. postcard commemorates the day the "wall came tumbling down," uniting Germany.

1990: Artist Ann Rusnak makes a political statement following the invasion of Kuwait by Saddam Hussein on August 2.

1991: Dogs, cats & National Postcard Week are the subjects of Sherry Kemp's design published by Memory Lane Postcards.

1992: Columbus' discovery voyage, depicted on Monumental Postcard Club's card by Carol Smith, was a hot topic in 1992.

CLUBS DIRECTORY

The purpose of this club roster is to provide contacts for prospective members or visitors who may wish to attend a meeting when in the area. Persons interested in participating in a local club are urged to contact the officers of a group near them.

Although meeting sites and times have been included, it's important to call ahead to verify this information for last-minute changes. Clubs are usually non-profit groups. If requesting a response in writing, be sure to include an SASE.

ALABAMA
Birmingham Post Card & Collectibles Club
Founded 1970
Bert Silman, Pres. & Memb.
3500 Pineland Dr., Birmingham, AL 35243
PH: 205-822-4375
Dues: $3.00
Homewood Public Library
1721 Oxmoor Rd., Birmingham, AL 35209
Third Thursday, 7:00pm
Annual Roster

ARIZONA
Arizona Post Card Club
Founded 1986
Bob Phelan, Pres. & Memb.
P.O. Box 40112, Phoenix, AZ 85067-0112
PH: 602-990-1007
Dues: $5.00
Villa Solano Clubhouse
5901 E. Thomas Rd., Phoenix, AZ
Second Wednesday, 7:00pm
Quarterly Newsletter, Annual Roster
Tucson Post Card Exchange Club
Founded 1990
Joan Gentry, Pres.
Stan Spurgiesz, Memb.
3338 E. Waverly St., Tucson, AZ 85716
PH: 602-325-1258, 602-297-0980
Dues: $10.00, $2.00 Additional Family Members
Call For Meeting Location
First Sunday, 2:00pm
Annual Roster, 6 Newsletters Per Year
Annual Show, January

ARKANSAS
Arkansas Postcard Club
Founded 1970
Jim Pfeifer, Pres.
15 Piedmont Lane, Little Rock, AR 72212
PH: 501-224-8887
Sam Storthz III, Memb.
20 Shannon Dr., Little Rock, AR 72207
Dues: $7.50, $10.00 Family
Bonanza Family Restaurant
109 E. Pershing, North Little Rock, AR
Second Thursday, 6:30pm
Monthly Newsletter, Annual Roster

CALIFORNIA
San Diego Postcard Club
Founded 1980
John & Jean Earl, Pres. & Memb.
1204 Madison Ave., San Diego, CA 92116-1031
Dues: $6.00, $7.00 Family
San Diego Public Library, Linda Vista Branch
2160 Ulric, San Diego, CA
Third Wednesday, 6:30pm
Newsletter
San Francisco Bay Area Postcard Club
Founded 1985
Jim Kurshuk, Memb.
1951 Eddy St., San Francisco, CA 94115
PH: 415-931-8936
Dues: $10.00, $12.00 Family, $15.00 Foreign
Fort Mason Center
Laguna & Marina Blvd., San Francisco, CA
Fourth Saturday Except December, 12:00noon-3:00pm
Annual Roster, 11 Newsletters Per Year
Special Events

San Jose Post Card Club
Founded 1985
Walter R. Kransky, Pres. & Memb.
P.O. Box 32628, San Jose, CA 95152
PH: 408-251-8304
Dues: $6.00, $13.00 Foreign
Rose Garden Library
1580 Naglee Ave., San Jose, CA
Second Tuesday, September Through June, 6:30-9:00pm
Annual Roster, Bimonthly Newsletter
Annual Show, Spring
Santa Cruz Post Card Club
Founded September 11, 1984
Joseph Jaynes, Pres.
2-1226 E. Cliff Dr., Santa Cruz, CA 95062
PH: 408-476-3262
Bonnie Nelson, Memb.
65 Leawood St., Aptos, CA 95003
Dues: $6.00
Capitola City Hall, Council Chambers
Capitola, CA
First Monday, 6:30pm
Monthly Newsletter, Annual Roster
Annual Show, April

Santa Monica Postcard Club
Lee Brown, Pres.
P.O. Box 92, Sunland, CA 91041
PH: 818-352-5663, 818-896-7919
Marshall Siskin, Memb.
1441 4th St., Santa Monica, CA 90401
Dues: $6.00, $1.00 Each Additional Family Member
Fairview Branch Library
2101 Ocean Park Blvd, Santa Monica, CA
First Thursday, 6:30pm
Monthly Meeting Notice, Call Dee Teitzell For Directions, 213-450-2665
Dealers & Sellers Welcome
Torrance-South Bay Post Card Collectors
Founded 1983
Doris L. Greene, Pres.
3205 Onrado St., Torrance, CA 90503-5932
PH: 310-328-8989
Oleta Whitecotton, Memb.
18509 Crenshaw Blvd., Torrance, CA 90504
PH: 310-329-8319
Dues: $6.00
Home Federal Bank
1670 Pacific Coast Hwy., Redondo Beach, CA
Last Sunday Except December, 2:00pm
Monthly Newsletter, Annual Roster For Attending Members

COLORADO
Denver Post Card Club
Founded September 1979
Robert Spencer, Pres.
4430 Gladiola St., Golden, CO 80403
PH: 303-279-4682
Carmen Schwartz, Memb.
P.O. Box 440068, Aurora, CO 80044
Dues: $6.00, $7.00 Family
South Gate Hall, Masonic Temple
15 E. Iowa Ave., Denver, CO
Third Sunday, 2:00pm
Bimonthly Newsletter, Annual Roster

CONNECTICUT
Connecticut Post Card Club
Founded 1954
Tom Dickau, Pres.
33 Fenway Ave., Bristol, CT 06010
Bill & Candie Callan, Memb.
340 Moose Hill Rd., Monroe, CT 06468

PH: 203-261-5058
Dues: $6.00, $4.00 Each Additional
   Family Member
Knights of Columbus Hall
2630 Whitney Ave., Hamden, CT
Third Sunday, 10:00am
Quarterly Newsletter, Annual Roster
Annual Show, April

FLORIDA

Sunshine Postcard Club
Lyn Friedt, Pres.
2236 Highland St. S., St. Petersburg, FL
   33705
PH: 813-823-4215
Dorothy Bruns, Memb.
210 6th Ave. N., St. Petersburg, FL
   33701
PH: 813-823-4060
Dues: $8.00, $2.00 Additional Family
   Members, $11.00 Canadian, $15.00
   Foreign
Holiday Inn-Stadium
4732 N. Dale Mabry, Tampa, FL
March 27, May 29, July 31, September
   25 (Mini Show), November 27,
   10:00am-4:00pm
Bimonthly Newsletter, 2 Shows Per
   Year, February & September
Club Address: P.O. Box 1232, St.
   Petersburg, FL 33731

Tropical Post Card Club
Founded 1979
Tom Moore, Pres.
6880 S.W. 75 Terrace, South Miami, FL
   33143
Wayne Kovacs, Memb.
10908 S.W. 135th Ct. Cir., Miami, FL
   33186
PH: 305-382-0398
Dues: $8.00, $2.00 Each Additional
   Family Member, $10.00 Canada,
   $16.00 Foreign
Royal Palm Clubhouse
545 N.E. 22nd Ave., Boynton Beach, FL
First Sunday, 12:00noon
Quarterly Newsletter, Annual Roster
2 Shows Per Year

GEORGIA

Georgia Postcard Club
Founded 1981
Don Woyce, Pres.
PH: 404-593-8305
Elnora Thurman, Memb.
3463 Holliglen Dr., Marietta, GA 30062
PH: 404-977-3263
Dues: $7.00 Family
Decatur Recreation Center
231 Sycamore St., Decatur, GA
Third Saturday, 11:00am-2:00pm
Bimonthly Bulletin, Annual Roster
2 Shows Per Year, Spring & Fall

ILLINOIS

Black Hawk Post Card Club
Founded 1980
Arretta Wetzel, Pres. & Memb.
1325 45 St., Rock Island, IL 61201
PH: 309-786-1335
Dues: $6.00, $1.00 Additional Family
   Members

Hauberg Civic Center
13th Ave. & 24th St., Rock Island, IL
Third Thursday Except August &
   December, 6:30pm
Newsletter, Annual Roster
Annual Show, March

Corn Belt Philatelic Society, Inc.
Mary Lynn Edwards, Pres.
Box 625, Bloomington, IL 61702-0625
Janice Jenkins, Memb.
Box 625, Bloomington, IL 61702-0625
PH: 309-663-2761
Dues: $6.00, $1.00 Each Additional
   Family Member
Champion Federal Savings & Loan
1501 E. College, Normal, IL 61761
Last Wednesday Except July Picnic &
   December, 7:00pm
Monthly Newsletter, Annual Show

Homewood Flossmoor Post Card Club
Founded 1977
Richard Barnes, Pres. & Memb.
P.O. Box 116, Hazel Crest, IL 60429
PH: 708-335-2735
Dues: $5.00, $7.50 Family
Dolphin Lake Clubhouse
183rd St. & Governors Highway,
   Homewood, IL
Second Tuesday, 7:30pm
10 Newsletters Per Year, Meeting Place
   Varies Occasionally
Annual Show, Second Saturday In
   October

Rock Valley Post Card Club
Founded 1983
Robert Swanson, Pres.
924 17th St., Rockford, IL 61104
PH: 815-398-5384
Molly Crocker, Memb.
P.O. Box 2722, Rockford, IL 61132-2722
PH: 815-282-5166
Dues: $5.00
Ken-Rock Community Center
3218 11th St., Rockford, IL 61109
First Monday, 7:00pm
Quarterly Newsletter
2 Shows Per Year, April & November

Windy City Post Card Club
John Belka, Pres.
P.O. Box 818, La Grange, IL 60525
Marianne Matthews, Memb.
P.O. Box 818, La Grange, IL 60525
Dues: $7.50, $3.50 Additional Family
   Members, $10.00 Foreign
Sokol Hall
3909 S. Prairie Ave., Brookfield, IL
Third Wednesday, 7:00pm
Bimonthly Newsletter, Bienniel Roster
Annual Show

INDIANA

Indianapolis Post Card Club
Founded 1974
Joseph Seiter, Pres.
2117 Winchester Dr., Indianapolis, IN
   46227
PH: 317-888-8475
Grace Perkoski, Memb.
3502 Moller Rd., Indianapolis, IN 46224
PH: 317-297-5611

Dues: $5.00, $6.00 Family
7th & 8th United Christian Church
2916 W. 30th/Medford, Indianapolis,
   IN
Second Thursday, 7:30pm
Bimonthly Bulletin, Annual Roster
Annual Show, Spring

Maple City Postcard Club
Founded 1969
Albert Hornberger, Pres.
218 River Vista Dr., Goshen, IN 46526
PH: 219-533-1340
Clara Reed, Memb.
2000 W. Wilden, Lot #136, Goshen, IN
   46526
First National Bank, Eastside Branch
2000 Middlebury St., Elkhart, IN
First Thursday, 7:30pm
Annual Show, March
Contact Thomas Zollinger, 219-522-
   3954, or Modern Postcards Sales,
   219-264-0013 for information.

Twin Bridges Postcard Club
Sarah Cooper, Pres.
Elsie Phillips, Memb.
536 S. Kerth Ave., Evansville, IN 47714
PH: 812-423-1811
Dues: $5.00
McCurdy Residential Center, Embers
   Room
101 SE 1st St., Evansville, IN
Second Monday, 6:00pm
Annual Roster, Annual Show

IOWA

Cedar Rapids Postcard Club
Founded February 1980
Wally Searcy, Pres.
3240 Whittier Rd., Springville, IA 52336
PH: 319-854-7359
Vivian Rinaberger, Sec./Treas.
4548 Fairlane Dr. NE, Cedar Rapids, IA
   52402
PH: 319-393-6743
Dues: $4.00, $7.00 Family
New Covenent Bible Church
1800 46 St. NE, Cedar Rapids, IA 52402
Third Thursday, 7:30pm
Bimonthly Newsletter, Annual Roster
2 Shows Per Year, May & October

Cheerio Post Card Club
Gladys Swaim, Memb.
Box 6, Webb, IA 51366
PH: 712-838-4365
Dues: $2.00
Public Library
Spencer, IA
Second Monday, 1:00pm

Hawkeye Postcard Club
Founded December 1978
Karen Hanley, Pres.
1161 21st St., W. Des Moines, IA 50265
PH: 515-224-0196
Agnes Aller, Memb.
2001 53rd St., Des Moines, IA 50310
PH: 515-279-5418
Dues: $5.00
Calvin West Apartments Activity Room
4210 Hickman Rd., Des Moines, IA
   50310

Third Thursday, 7:00pm
Quarterly Newsletter, Annual Roster
Annual Show, 4th Saturday In
    September
Iowa Wildrose Postcard Club
David A. Wilson, Pres.
836 Lynkaylee Dr., Waterloo, IA 50701
PH: 319-232-2506
Laura Fox, Memb.
721 2nd Ave., Evansdale, IA 50707
PH: 319-235-1194
Various Meeting Sites
Third Monday, 7:00pm
Post Card Pals
Founded 1972
Betty Weiland, Pres. & Memb.
2324 Maplewood Dr., Dubuque, IA 52001
PH: 319-583-8342
Emmaus Bible College
2570 Asbury, Dubuque, IA
Second Thursday, 7:00pm
KANSAS
Wichita Postcard Club
Founded 1977
Hal Ottaway, Pres.
P.O. Box 780282, Wichita, KS 67278-0282
PH: 316-686-5574
Dorothy L. Johnson, Memb.
P.O. Box 780282, Wichita, KS 67278-0282
Dues: $8.00, $1.00 Each Additional
    Family Member, $15.00 Foreign
Wichita Public Library
South Main, Wichita, KS
Alternating Between First Tuesday
    Evening & First Saturday Afternoon
    Each Month
Monthly Newsletter With Free Ads For
    Members, Annual Roster
Annual Auction, April
Annual Swap Meet, June
Annual Show, October
Annual NPW, Membership & Show
    Postcards by Rick Geary
MAINE
Pine Tree Post Card Club
Founded 1978
Joseph LePage, Pres.
P.O. Box 6815, Portland, ME 04101
Earl Tibbetts, Memb.
P.O. Box 6815, Portland, ME 04101
PH: 207-775-2716
Dues: $5.00
Portland Public Safety Bldg.
109 Middle St., Portland, ME
Second Monday, 7:00pm
Quarterly Newsletter
3 Shows Per Year, May, July, October
MARYLAND
Capitol Beltway Postcard Club
Founded 1976
Tony Chaves, Pres. & Memb.
P.O. Box 366, Falls Church, VA 22040
PH: 703-560-0237
Dues: $8.00, $10.00 Couple, $30.00 Dealer
Greenbelt Middle School
8950 Edmonston Rd., Greenbelt, MD
Second Thursday Except July &
    August, 6:30pm
Bimonthly Newsletter, Annual Roster

Maryland Postcard Society
Founded 1992
Dee Delcher, Memb.
413 E. Lake Ave., Baltimore, MD 21212
PH: 410-433-1532
3 Shows Per Year, May, September,
    December
Show Program
Monumental Postcard Club
John Corliss, Pres.
Sandy Waters, Memb.
3013 St. Paul St., Baltimore, MD 21218
Dues: $8.00 Single, $10.00 Family,
    $20.00 Foreign
Star Community Hall
7405 Windsor Mill Rd., Baltimore, MD
    21207
4th Sunday Except July, August &
    December, 1:00-5:00pm
9 Newssheets Per Year, Annual Roster
Annual Show, October

MASSACHUSETTS
Bay State Post Card Collectors' Club
Founded 1948
John J. Vierra, Pres.
P.O. Box 6783, Portland, ME 04101
PH: 207-657-4399
Anne E. Crane, Memb. & Corr. Sec.
P.O. Box 334, Lexington, MA 02173
PH: 617-646-3576
Dues: $7.00
Elks Hall
37 Florence St., Malden, MA 02148
Second Sunday Except April, July &
    August, 9:00am-3:30pm
Bimonthly "Post Card Digest," Biennial
    Roster
Annual Show, April

Cape Cod Post Card Collectors Club
Founded 1985
Sue Beyle, Pres.
P.O. Box 946, North Eastham, MA
    02651
PH: 508-255-3389
Helen Angell, Memb.
Short Neck Rd., So. Dennis, MA 02660
PH: 508-398-1793
Dues: $5.00
Carlton Hall
Old Bass River Rd., Dennis, MA
Last Thursday Except July, August &
    September, 6:30pm
Quarterly Newsletter
Annual Show, September
Central Massachusetts Post Card Club
Founded 1983
Gerald Blanchard Jr., Pres.
132 Colonial Dr., Athol, MA 01331
Nancy Waddell, Memb.
10 Mary Anna Dr., Fitchburg, MA
    01420
PH: 508-342-3221
Dues: $7.00
Barre Legion Post #2
Mechanic St., Barre, MA 01945
Last Wednesday Except July, Aug,
    Dec., 7:00pm
Annual Roster, 6 Newsletters Per Year
Annual Show, November
MICHIGAN
Southwest Michigan Post Card Club
Founded 1976
Joy Miller, Pres.
3919 Hayes, Portage, MI 49081
PH: 616-327-8005
Stanley Smeed, Memb.
1419 Baker Dr., Kalamazoo, MI 49001
PH: 616-344-5304
Dues: $2.00
Meeting Locations Vary, Call for
    Information
First Monday, 7:00pm
Annual Roster
2 Shows Per Year, April & October
Wolverine Postcard Club
Founded September 1954
Milton Schleicher, Pres.
46555 North Ave., Mt. Clemens, MI
    48045
PH: 313-949-2672
Laura N. Goldberg, Memb.
1313 E. Harry, Hazel Park, MI 48030
PH: 313-545-8552
Dues: $7.00, $1.00 Additional Family
    Members, $4.00 Junior Members
Laura Goldberg Home
1313 E. Harry, Hazel Park, MI 48030
Second Saturday, 12:00noon
Quarterly Bulletin, Annual Roster
MINNESOTA
Twin City Postcard Club
Founded: 1976
Adina M. Overbee, Pres.
P.O. Box 39513, Minneapolis, MN 55439
David Johnson, Memb.
P.O. Box 39513, Minneapolis, MN 55439
PH: 612-426-3573

Dues: $9.00, $1.00 Each Additional
    Family Member
Richfield Community Center
70th St. & Nicollet Ave. S., Richfield,
    MN 39513
Third Wednesday Except July &
    December, 6:45pm
Monthly Bulletin, Annual Roster
2 Shows Per Year, March & September

MISSOURI

Gateway Postcard Club
Founded 1974
Fred Longshaw, Pres.
Kathy Danielsen, Memb.
P.O. Box 1208, O'Fallon, IL 62269
PH: 618-632-1921
Dues: $7.00
Kirkwood Community Center
111 Geyer Rd., Kirkwood, MO
First Monday Except September,
    7:30pm
Quarterly Newsletter, Biennial Roster
2 Shows Per Year, Spring & Fall

Heart of America Postcard Collectors
Founded 1982
Henry Heflin, Pres.
Don E. Harmon, Memb.
12806 W. 71st, Shawnee, KS 66216
PH: 913-268-6149
Dues: $7.50
All Souls Unitarian Church
4500 Warwick, Kansas City, MO
Third Tuesday, February, March, April,
    September, October, November,
    7:00pm
6 Newsletters Per Year, Annual Roster
Annual Show, May

68 ✳

**Mark Twain Postcard Club of the Tri-
State Area**
Founded September 1991
Steve Chou, Pres.
Rt. 2, Box 85, New London, MO 63459
PH: 314-221-0066
Sally Polc, Memb.
24 Brown Estates, Hannibal, MO 63401
PH: 314-248-1216
Dues: $10.00, payable in September
Farm & Home Savings Bldg.
190 Huck Finn Shopping Center,
    Hannibal, MO 63401
Second Thursday, 6:30pm
Monthly Newsletter, Annual Show, July
Auction, Presentation, Swap & Sell At
    Monthly Meetings

MONTANA

Montana Post Card & Paper Club
Founded 1986
Tom Mulvaney, Pres. & Memb.
Box 814, East Helena, MT 59635
PH: 406-227-8790
Dues: $5.00
2 Newsletters Per Year, Roster Included
2 Shows Per Year

NEBRASKA

Lincoln Postcard Club
Founded 1986
Jerry Pettit, Pres. & Memb.
25413 Mill Rd., Greenwood, NE 68366
PH: 402-867-2924
Dues: $6.00
Holiday Inn Northeast
5250 Cornhusker Hwy., Lincoln, NE
Third Thursday Except July &
    December, 7:30pm
Newsletter, Annual Roster
1-Day Show, June

NEW HAMPSHIRE

Granite State Postcard Collectors Club
Founded 1983
David Sysyn, Pres.
Box 341, Hancock, NH 03449
PH: 603-827-3654
Gladys Morabito, Corr. Sec.
P.O. Box 109, Rumney, NH 03266
PH: 603-786-9333
Dues: $7.00, $14.00 Foreign
Unitarian Church
Central St., Franklin, NH 03235
Third Saturday, 9:00am
Monthly Newsletter, 3 Gazettes Per
    Year, Annual Roster
2 Shows Per Year

NEW JERSEY

Central Jersey Deltiological Society
Founded 1981
Patricia McDorman, Pres.
Norman Bobel, Memb.
518 Front St., Dunellen, NJ 08812
PH: 908-968-4249
Dues: $6.00
Knights Of Columbus Hall
Grove St. & South Ave., Dunellen, NJ
    08812
Third Sunday Except If Easter &

August (Second Sunday), 1:00pm
Monthly Newsletter, Annual Roster,
    Quarterly Journal
Annual Show, Saturday Before Third
    Sunday In August

Garden State Post Card Collectors Club
Founded 1959
Irving Dolin, Pres.
Dolores Kirchgessner, Memb.
421 Washington St., Hoboken, NJ 07030
PH: 201-659-1922
Dues: $5.00, $4.00 Additional Members
Berkeley Heights Recreation Center
56 Columbus Ave., Berkeley Heights, NJ
First Sunday Except October, 12:00noon
Periodic Newsletter, Annual Roster
Annual Show, October

South Jersey Post Card Club
Founded 1971
David B. Grubbs, Pres.
212 Kathy Dr., Yardley, PA 18067
Alex Antal, Memb.
#4 Plymouth Dr., Marlton, NJ 08053
PH: 609-983-1450
Dues: $6.00, $9.00 Family
Holiday Inn
Runnemede, NJ
Second Sunday Except April, 1:00pm
Quarterly Bulletin, Monthly Newsletter,
    Roster $1.00
Annual Show, April

NEW YORK

Buffalo Postcard Club
Edward H. Small, Jr., Pres.
992 Virginia Dr., Alden, NY 14004
PH: 716-937-6763
Ken Butts, Memb.
97 Fairhaven Dr., Cheektowaga, NY
    14225
PH: 716-634-5970
Dues: $7.00 First Year, $5.00 Thereafter
Cleveland Heights Christian Church
4774 Union Rd., Cheektowaga, NY
    14225
First Tuesday, 7:00pm
Annual Show, March

Central New York Post Card Club
Founded May 1977
Sandra J. Drake, Pres.
R.D.2, Box 144, Canastota, NY 13032
PH: 315-697-7330
Ruth R. Weimer, Memb.
R.D.2, Box 173, RTE. 31, Canastota, NY
    13032
PH: 315-697-7157
Dues: $8.00, $10.00 Couple
Clinton, Oneida, & Little York Lake
Call For Meeting Dates
12:00noon
Quarterly Bulletin, Annual Roster
2 Shows Per Year, Spring & Fall

Corning-Painted Post Postcard Society
Founded 1977
Gertrude Boland, Pres. & Memb.
136 High Rd., Corning, NY 14830
Dues: None
Public Library
Nasser Plaza, Corning, NY 14830
Second Thursday, 7:00pm

Kaaterskill Post Card Club, Inc.
Founded 1975
Donald Stephens, Pres.
P.O. Box 177, Glenford, NY 12433
PH: 914-657-2036
Eric Fedde, Memb.
RD 1, Box 418A, Stone Ridge, NY 12484
PH: 914-687-7555
Dues: $5.00, $6.00 Family, $10.00
    Foreign
Hurley Reformed Church
Main St., Hurley, NY
First Wednesday, 7:30pm
Monthly Newsletter, Annual Roster
3 Shows Per Year

Long Island Postcard Club
Founded 1977
Rikki Springsteed, Pres.
Eric Karlson, Memb.
228 Oakland Ave., Central Islip, NY 11722
PH: 516-342-0421
Dues: $7.00, $10.00 Family
Good Shepherd Lutheran Church
Hempstead Turnpike, Levittown, NY
First Thursday Except July & August,
    6:30-9:30pm
Quarterly Bulletin, Annual Roster
Annual Show, Spring

Metropolitan Post Card Club
Founded 1946
Leah Schnall, Pres. & Memb.
67-00 192nd St., Flushing, NY 11365
PH: 718-454-0582
Dues: $10.00
Days Inn
440 W. 57th St., New York, NY 10019
Second Sunday Except May & Novem-
    ber, 10:00am
Bimonthly Newsletter, Biennial Roster
2 Shows Per Year, May & November

Post Card Club Of Oswego County
Founded 1981
Barbara Wilshire, Pres.
RD. 6, Box 92, Oswego, NY 13126
PH: 315-343-4923
Lillian McCloskey, Memb.
7 West 8th St., Oswego, NY 13126
PH: 315-343-1049
Dues: $3.00, $5.00 Family
Roy McCrobie Bldg.
Lake St., Oswego, NY 13126
Second Wednesday, October-June,
    7:00pm
2 Newsletters Per Year, Annual Show

Upstate New York Post Card Club
Founded 1972
James Davis, Pres.
5 Cutter Dr., Johnstown, NY 12095
PH: 518-762-8659
Dorothy Baron, Memb.
1832 Fiero Ave., Schenectady, NY 12303
PH: 518-355-5885
Dues: $4.00
Second Presbyterian Church
25 Church St., Amsterdam, NY 12010
Second Friday Except July &
    September, 7:00pm
Annual Roster, 6 Bulletins Per Year
Annual Show, September

Western New York Postcard Club
Founded 1975
John Williams, Pres.
7217 Lake Ave., Williamson, NY 14589
PH: 315-589-8400
William A. Ruth, Memb.
7421 E. Main St., Lima, NY 14485
PH: 716-624-4160
Dues: $8.00, $10.00 Family
Carmen Clark Lodge
Brighton Town Park, 777 Westfall Rd.,
    Rochester, NY 14618
Third Sunday, 12:00noon
Quarterly Bulletin, Annual Roster
Annual Show, Fall

NORTH CAROLINA

Tarheel Postcard Club
Founded 1978
Jay Patel, Pres.
2500 Battleground Ave., Greensboro,
    NC 27408
PH: 919-288-0122
Caroline Cornish, Memb.
314 N. Elam, Greensboro, NC 27403
Dues: $5.00, $8.00 Family
Meeting Site:
5307 Thorncliff Dr., Greensboro, NC
    27410
Floating Saturdays Except July &
    August, 1:00pm
Annual Roster, 10 Newsletters Per
    Year

OHIO

Greater Cincinnati Post Card Club
Founded 1983
George Budd, Pres.
6910 Tenderfoot Lane, Cincinnati, OH
    45249
PH: 513-489-0518
Al Wettstein, Memb.
23-90 8 Mile Rd., Cincinnati, OH 45244
PH: 513-474-0855
Dues: $4.00
Brookwood Retirement Community
12100 Reed Hartman Hwy., Cincinnati,
    OH 45241
Second Sunday Except June, July &
    August, 2:00pm

Heart of Ohio Post Card Club
Founded 1975
Jim Davis, Pres.
2639 Alder Vista Dr., Columbus, OH
    43231
PH: 614-891-0020
Mrs. Philomena George, Memb.
1701 East Cooke Rd., Columbus, OH
    43224-2110
PH: 614-268-7622
Dues: $5.00, $7.50 Couple
Chemical Abstract
Olentangy River Rd., Columbus, OH
Second Thursday, 7:00pm
Quarterly Newsletter, Annual Roster
Three Shows Per Year

Johnny Appleseed Postcard Club, Inc.
Founded July 13, 1973
John Wagenhals, Pres.
P.O. Box 801, Ashland, OH 44805

PH: 419-281-1997
Frances Dunnigan, Sec.
P.O. Box 801, Ashland, OH 44805
PH: 419-281-3340
Dues: $5.00, $7.50 Family
Pic-A-Deli Restaurant
4 East Main St., Ashland, OH 44805
First Monday Except January &
    February, Second Monday When
    First Is Holiday, 7:00pm
10 Newsletters Per Year
Annual Show, June

Tri-County Postcard Club
Founded March 1990
Ray Ferrell, Pres. & Memb.
332 St. Clair Ave., Cadiz, OH 43907
PH: 614-942-3475
Dues: $6.00
Presbyterian Church
633 N. Main St., Uhrichsville, OH
Second Monday, 7:00pm
Annual Show, First Weekend In April

Western Reserve Post Card Society
Founded 1973
Paul Knapp, Pres.
25028 Rainbow Dr., Olmsted Falls, OH
    44138
PH: 216-234-4441
Shirley Goldberg, Memb.
2673 Cranlyn Rd., Cleveland, OH 44122
Dues: $7.00
Lenau Park
7370 Columbia Rd., Rt. 252, Olmsted
    Falls, OH 44138
Third Saturday Except July & August,
    10:00am
8 Newsletters Per Year, Biennial Roster
Annual Show, May

OKLAHOMA

T-Town Postcard Club
Founded 1981
Ken Miller, Pres.
P.O. Box 700334, Tulsa, OK 74170
Charlie Williams, Memb.
P.O. Box 700334, Tulsa, OK 74170
Dues: $6.00, $1.00 Additional Family
    Members
Eastland Mall Community Center
145th East Ave. & 21st St., Tulsa, OK
First Tuesday, 7:00pm
10 Newsletters Per Year, Call 918-743-
    1854 For Information
Annual Show, May

OREGON

Southern Oregon Philatelic Society
Founded 1951
Donald Cramer, Pres.
717 Broad St., Medford, OR 97501
PH: 503-779-4671
Elsie Sterton, Memb.
59 Summit, Medford, OR 97501
PH: 503-772-7209
Dues: $7.50
Presbyterian Church
85 S. Holly, Medford, OR
First Thursday, 7:30pm
2 Shows Per Year, April & October
Postal History Study Group

Webfooters Post Card Club
Founded 1966
Terry Weis, Pres.
HCR-61, Box 78J, Banks, OR 97106
PH: 503-324-0970
Mona I. Campbell, Memb.
13025 S.W. Grant Ave., Tigard, OR
  97223-5101
PH: 503-639-1507
Dues: $8.00, $8.50 Family
Sunnyside Masonic Temple
3862 S.E. Hawthorne Blvd., Portland,
  OR
Third Saturday, 10:00am-5:00pm
Quarterly Bulletin, Annual Roster
Annual Shows

Willamette Valley Post Card Club
Founded June 1991
Cathy Clark, Chm.
P.O. Box 135, Lake Oswego, OR 97034
PH: 503-697-6576 (day)
Mike Hebrank, Memb.
P.O. Box 68146, Portland, OR 97268
PH: 503-654-7119 (eve)
Dues: $10.00 Single Or Family, $6.00
  "Living Lightly"
Oak Grove Community Club
14496 S.E. Cedar St., Oak Grove, OR
Second Saturday Except July & August,
  11:00am Educational Workshop,
  12:00 Bourse
Educational Workshops, Workshop
  Summaries To Members
Annual Show, Second Saturday In
  September

PENNSYLVANIA
Anthracite Postcard Club
Founded 1987
Norm Brauer, Pres.
114 W. Main St., Dalton, PA 18414
Connie Horn, Memb.
Box 102 Rd. #1, New Milford, PA 18834
Dues: $5.00
Clarks Summit Boro Hall
Clarks Summit, PA 18411
Second Sunday Except Summer,
  7:00pm
Bimonthly Newsletter, Annual Roster

Greater Johnstown Postcard Club
Founded 1982
Tom Shook, Pres.
724 Bucknell Ave., Johnstown, PA
  15905
PH: 814-535-4686
Carole Barto, Memb.
1097-1/2 Edson Ave., Johnstown, PA
  15905
PH: 814-535-2369
Dues: $5.00, $8.00 Family
Pittsburgh National Bank Community
  Room
Market St., Johnstown, PA
Third Thursday Except August &
  December, 7:00pm
Annual Roster, Annual Newsletter
Annual Show, October

Lancaster County Postcard Club
Founded 1990
Don Davis, Pres.
61 W. Cottage Ave., Millersville, PA
  17551
PH: 717-872-8630
Sally Danz, Memb.
65 Greenwood Ave., Lancaster, PA
  17603
PH: 717-397-4602
Dues: $7.00, $10.00 Family
Faith United Church of Christ
1204 Wabank St., Lancaster, PA
Third Monday, 7:00pm
Monthly Newsletter
Correspondence To Box 300, Lititz, PA
  17543-0300

Lehigh Valley Post Card Club
Founded 1983
Ray Holland, Pres.
2020 Hamilton St., Allentown, PA
  18104
PH: 215-439-4855
R.F. Kichline, Memb.
P.O. Box 3008, Palmer, PA 18043
Dues: $5.00, $7.00 Family
Holiday Hairfashions Auditorium
2020 Hamilton St., Allentown, PA
Third Tuesday, 6:30pm
Monthly Newsletter Except December,
  Annual Roster
Annual Show, October

Morlatton Postcard Club
Founded 1975
Leon Rowe, Pres.
123 Magnolia St., Kennet Square, PA
  19348
PH: 215-444-0641
Kay Feight, Memb.
806 Stanley Ave., Chambersburg, PA
  17201-2838
PH: 717-263-1638
Dues: $5.00, $6.00 Family
2 Shows Per Year, Spring & Fall

Pocono Postcard Collectors Club
Bob Kaiser, Pres.
Emily Carter, Memb.
279 Locust Ridge Rd., Pocono Lake, PA
  18347
PH: 717-646-2879
Dues: $3.00
Trail's End Cafe
Delaware Water Gap, PA 18327
Third Saturday, 7:30pm
Monthly Newsletter

Susquehanna Valley Postcard Club
Founded 1982
Roy Shoop, Pres.
P.O. Box 132, Northumberland, PA
  17857
Ralph Vanderbeck, Memb.
P.O. Box 132, Northumberland, PA
  17857
Dues: $5.00, $1.00 Additional Family
  Members

Hunter Mansion Museum
N. Front St. (Rear), Sunbury, PA
Last Sunday, 6:00pm Bourse, 7:30pm
  Meeting
Monthly Newsletter, Annual Roster
Annual Show, June

3 Rivers Postcard Club
George Smurlo, Pres.
Richard Campbell, Memb.
Box 25313, Pittsburgh, PA 15242
Dues: $6.00
Mt. Lebanon Methodist Church
3319 W. Liberty Ave., Mt. Lebanon, PA
Third Wednesday, 7:30pm
Annual Newsletter & Roster

**Washington Crossing Card Collectors
Club**
Founded 1972
Vernon Wersler, Pres.
P.O. Box 39, Washington Crossing, PA
  18977
PH: 215-345-0408
David Grubbs, Memb.
P.O. Box 39, Washington Crossing, PA
  18977
PH: 215-493-0618
Dues: $7.00, $8.00 Family, $9.00
  Foreign, $5.00 Junior
Titusville Presbyterian Church
River Dr., Titusville, NJ 08560
Second Monday, 8:00pm
Monthly Bulletin, Annual Roster

York Post Card Club
Founded 1989
Dick Kestenbaum, Pres.
P.O. Box 173, York, PA 17405-0173
Richard Bishop, Memb.
P.O. Box 173, York, PA 17405-0173
Dues: $8.00, $10.00 Family
York Valley Inn
3883 E. Market St., York, PA
Second Monday, 6:00pm Dealer Sales,
  7:30pm General Meeting
Monthly Newsletter, 4 Postcards Per
  Year
Annual Show, July

RHODE ISLAND
Rhode Island Post Card Club
Founded May 25, 1958
Thomas A. Hawk, Pres.
230 Orchard St., Cranston, RI 02910
PH: 401-941-6884
Evelyn M. Marshall, Memb.
37 Ryder Ave., Apt. #2, Cranston, RI
  02920-5409
Dues: $9.00, Includes Family/Associate
  Residing In Same Household
Knights Of Columbus Hall
1 New Road, Rumford, RI
Last Sunday Except July & August,
  8:00am-4:00pm
Bimonthly Bulletin Except July &
  August, Biannual Roster
Annual Show, Last Sunday In October,
  Site & Chairperson Determined In
  Spring

SOUTH CAROLINA
South Carolina Post Card Collectors Club
Founded April 9, 1983
Davie Beard, Pres.
1809 Brevard Pl., Camden, SC 29020
PH: 803-432-2854
Wayne Porter, Memb.
P.O. Box 10648, Rock Hill, SC 29731-0648
PH: 803-324-5820
Dues: $5.00, $1.00 Additional Family Members
Various Cities
Saturday Four Times Per Year, 10:00am-3:00pm
Newsletter Before Each Meeting, Annual Roster
Annual Show, First Week In September After Labor Day

TENNESSEE
East Tennessee Postcard Club
Founded 1989
Milton Hinshilwood, Pres.
3724 Keowee Ave., Knoxville, TN 37919
PH: 615-525-7370
Elena I. Zimmerman, Memb.
7914 Gleason Dr. #1061, Knoxville, TN 37919
PH: 615-690-6469
Dues: $6.00, $7.00 Couples
Clubhouse
7914 Gleason Dr., Knoxville, TN 37919
Fourth Saturday, 11:00am
Annual Roster

TEXAS
Capital Of Texas Post Card Club
Founded 1990
Bill Bassett, Pres.
P.O. Box 202471, Austin, TX 78720
PH: 512-335-1300
Kathy Fesler, Memb.
P.O. Box 202471, Austin, TX 78720
PH: 512-260-2630
Dues: $8.00, $1.00 Additional Family Members
Windows To The Past
5525 Burnet Ave., Austin, TX 78756
Second Sunday, 2:00pm
Quarterly Bulletin, Annual Roster
Annual Show

Cowtown Post Card Club
Founded 1954
James McMillin, Pres.
3306 Ave. D, Ft. Worth, TX 76105
PH: 817-535-3961
Ruth Scott, Memb.
1615 Bluebonnet Dr., Fort Worth, TX 76111
PH: 817-834-0103
Dues: $5.00, $6.00 Family
Members' Homes
Third Sunday, 2:00pm
Annual Roster
Annual Show, July Or August

Dallas Metroplex Postcard Club
Founded 1983
Leroy King, Jr., Pres.
4815 Allencrest, Dallas, TX 75244
PH: 214-239-1280
Larry W. Seymour, Memb.
822 SE 8th St., Grand Prairie, TX 75051
PH: 214-264-0723
Dues: $6.00
Farmers Branch Manske Library
13613 Webb Chapel, Farmers Branch, TX 75234
Saturday, 1:00pm
Annual Roster, Monthly Bulletin Announcing Meeting Date
Annual Show, March

Greater Houston Postcard Society
Sherry Roberson, Pres.
733 Winding Rd., Pasadena, TX 77504
PH: 713-944-1098
Mary Chapman, Memb.
4816 Palmetto, Bellaire, TX 77401
PH: 713-461-1374
Dues: $6.00, $2.50 Additional Family Members, $7.50 Foreign
Call For Meeting Location
Second Sunday Except Summer, 2:00-5:00pm
Quarterly Newsletter, Annual Roster
Annual Show, October

Houston Post Card Club
Founded October 17, 1977
Gloria Grolla, Pres.
1616 Park Haven, Houston, TX 77077
PH: 713-589-1873
Devon Hart, Memb.
8502 Woodcamp, Houston, TX 77088
PH: 713-999-3936
Dues: $6.00, $7.00 Family, $3.00 Junior
Rice Epicurean Market, Community Room
6425 San Felipe, Houston, TX
Third Sunday, 2:00pm
5 Newsletters Per Year, Annual Roster
Annual Show, March

UTAH
Utah Postcard Collectors Club
Founded 1986
Dennis Goreham, Pres. & Memb.
1539 East 4070 South, Salt Lake City, UT 84124
PH: 801-277-5119
Lamar Peterson, Memb.
Stan Sander's Bottle Museum
2743 South Blair St. (360 East), Salt Lake City, UT
Fourth Thursday, 7:00pm
Monthly Newsletter

VIRGINIA
NOVA Postcard Club
John McClintock, Pres. & Memb.
P.O. Box 1765, Manassas, VA 22110
PH: 703-368-2757
Dues: 50 cents/meeting
Manassas School Of Dance, Manassas Shopping Center
Mathis Ave., Manassas, VA
Third Sunday Except July & August, 1:00pm

Old Dominion Postcard Club
Founded 1978
Jim Adams, Vice Pres.
9302 Lyndon Way Dr., Richmond, VA 23229
PH: 804-346-4938
Art Seidenberg, Memb.
PH: 804-353-4434
Dues: $8.00, $10.00 Family
Signet Bank Bldg.
N. 8th & E. Main St., Richmond, VA 23219
Second Tuesday, 7:00pm
Monthly Newsletter
Annual Show, November

WASHINGTON
Pacific Northwest Post Card Club
Founded August 6, 1980
Bary Bender, Pres.
Rich Klepac, Memb.
28828 207th S.E., Kent, WA 98042
PH: 206-630-2012
Dues: $6.00, $9.00 Canada, $17.00 Foreign
Lake City Community Center
12531 28th Ave. NE, Seattle, WA 98125
First Sunday Except July & August, 12:00noon
Bimonthly Bulletin, Annual Roster
2 Shows Per Year, January & June

WISCONSIN
Four Lakes Postcard Club
Founded 1988
Joe Stransky, Pres.
P.O. Box 1672, Madison, WI 53704
PH: 608-877-0531
Ann Waidelich, Memb.
2150 Lakeland Ave., Madison, WI 53704
PH: 608-249-7920
Dues: $3.00
Immanuel Lutheran Church
1021 Spaight St., Madison, WI 53703
Fourth Tuesday, 7:30pm
Annual Roster
Annual Show, January

Milwaukee Post Card Collectors Club
Founded 1977
Robert Koehler, Pres.
P.O. Box 10153, Milwaukee, WI 53210
PH: 414-442-4700
John Ford, Memb.
P.O. Box 10153, Milwaukee, WI 53210
Dues: $5.00
Forest Home Library
1432 W. Forest Home Ave., Milwaukee, WI
First Monday, 7:00pm
Quarterly Newsletter, Annual Roster
2 Shows Per Year, April & October

CANADA
Golden Horseshoe Post Card Club
Founded 1985
Paul McWhinnie, Pres.
Louise Kaye, Memb.
P.O. Box 66660, Stony Creek, ONT,

Canada L8G 5E6
PH: 416-957-7227
Dues: $5.00, $1.00 Each Additional
    Family Member
Burlington Spectator Bldg.
534 Brant St., Burlington, ONT, Canada
Fourth Wednesday Except July,
    August, December, 7:30pm
Annual Roster, 3 Newsletters Per Year
Annual Show, Fall

Toronto Postcard Club
Founded 1977
Bob McEvilla, Pres.
P.O. Box 6184, Postal Station A,
    Toronto, ONT, Canada M5W 1P6
Diana Davies, Memb.
P.O. Box 6184, Postal Station A,
    Toronto, ONT, Canada M5W 1P6
Dues: $15.00, $20.00 U.S., $25.00
    Foreign
Agincourt Collegiate Institute, Room
    114
Midland Ave., Scarborough, Ontario,
    Canada
2nd & 4th Thursday Except July &
    August & 4th Thursday June &
    December, 8:00pm
3 Newsletters Per Year, Annual Roster
Annual Show, Last Sunday In February

Vancouver Post Card Club
Founded 1981
Albert Tanner, Pres.
#201-1025 Gilford St., Vancouver, BC,
    Canada V6G 2P2
PH: 604-685-0383
Ron Souch, Memb.
#20-1201 Lamey's Mill Rd., Vancouver,
    BC, Canada
PH: 604-731-1481
Dues: $12.00
Hastings Community Centre
3096 E. Hastings St., Vancouver, BC,
    Canada V5K 2A3
Third Tuesday Except July & August,
    7:00pm
5 Newsletters Per Year
Annual Show, June

MAIL CLUBS
**Association of Map Memorabilia
    Collectors**
Founded 1986
Siegfried Feller, Memb.
8 Amherst Rd., Pelham, MA 01002
PH: 413-253-3115
Dues: $12.50 U.S. & Canada, $17.00
    Foreign
Quarterly Newsletter "Cartomania"

Cosmopolitan Post Card Club
Frank Pichardo, Memb.
P.O. Box 1116, Flushing, NY 11354-0035
PH: 718-359-1183
Dues: $15.00/Two Years
Annual Roster, 8 Bulletins Per Year

Curt Teich Postcard Archives
Founded 1982
Christine Pyle, Memb.
Lake Co. Museum, Lakewood Forest
    Preserve, Wauconda, IL 60084

PH: 708-526-8638
Dues: $20.00
Quarterly Journal, Postcard Exhibit
10% Membership Discount On Re-
    search Services

Deltiologists of America
Founded 1960
Dr. James Lewis Lowe, Dir.
P.O. Box 8, Norwood, PA 19074
Bimonthly Newsletter "Postcard
    Classics" (Sample Copy $3.00)
Information Available (Long SASE, 2
    First Class Stamps)

Garfield Gang Post Card Club
Founded February 14, 1986
Joan B. Carlson, Pres. & Memb.
905 Route 163, Oakdale, CT 06370
Dues: $3.00
Quarterly Newsletter, Auction

Gay Philatelic/Postcard Society
Founded 1981
Ed S. Centeno, Pres. & Memb.
Box 230940, Hartford, CT 06123-0940
Dues: $6.00
Lambda Philatelic Journal, Roster
NYC Show, June

Horse Collectors Of America
Founded 1987
Gail Nixon, Pres. & Memb.
6220 Penrose Ave., Dallas, TX 75214-
    3040
PH: 214-823-2160
Dues: $7.00
Annual Roster, 4 Newsletters Per Year

**International Disney Post Card
    Collectors Club**
Founded May 1987
Jay Patel, Memb.
2500 Battleground Ave., Greensboro,

NC 27408
Dues: $5.00, $6.00 Canada, $8.00
    Foreign
Quarterly Newsletter, Annual Roster
1993 Show Card Free To Members

International Postcard Exchange
Founded January 1992
Jennifer Batt, Pres. & Memb.
7960 N.W. 50th St., #108, Lauderhill, FL
    33351
PH: 305-746-8585
Dues: $5.00 U.S., $5.00 Worth of
    Postcards Foreign
Annual Roster
Membership Open To Collectors &
    Dealers Worldwide

Maximum Card Study Unit
E. Clark Buchi, Pres.
P.O. Box 453, Brentwood, TN 37024-
    0453
Gary Dennis, Memb.
P.O. Box 11447, Norfolk, VA 23517
Dues: $10.00, $15.00 Foreign
Quarterly Newsletter

**Organization For Collectors of
    Covered Bridge Postcards**
Kay Lloyd, Pres.
7 Squantum St., Milton, MA 02186
Linda Jane Willauer, Memb.
110 Shady Lane, Fayetteville, NY 13066
Dues: $4.00
Bimonthly Bulletin, Annual Roster

Postcard History Society
Founded 1975
John McClintock, Dir. & Memb.
P.O. Box 1765, Manassas, VA 22110
PH: 703-368-2757
Dues: $5.00
Quarterly Illustrated Bulletin

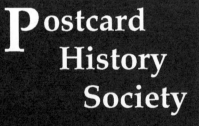

1992

Customer Service Award Recipients

Antique Paper Guild
Butterfield & Butterfield
Card Collector's Co.
Card Shark
Carlton's Modern Postcards
Colonial House
Columbus Productions
Delcher, Dee
Gray, Harris
Green Dragon
Ham's Cards
Hodapp, Sue
Jameison Postcards & Antiques
Jerry's Cards
Kaye, Donald
La Posta Publications
Landmark Postcards
Majorstamps
Martin, Ltd., Mary
Mc Clintock Postcard Sales

Michael Bennett Auctions
Millns, Sandy & John
Modern Postcard Sales
Moulton, Alison & Richard
National Postcard Exchange
Nicholson, Susan
Novick, Richard
Numismatic Card Co.
Prag, Ken
Rodriguez, Jose
Zinzermatic Productions

5 Year Recipients

Bowers, Dave
Dobres, Sheldon
Grab Bag Antiques
Schryver, Jane
Shiloh Postcards

The **Customer Service Award** is an acknowledged symbol of honesty and integrity in postcard dealing and is based on the following criteria:

- No complaints outstanding at the end of 1992 and no more than two complaints registered during the year;
- All test order materials received as described;
- Display ads appeared in at least four issues during 1992;
- Display advertising space accumulated to at least 40 column inches during 1992* (* Some restrictions apply);
- All advertising paid in full;
- And other criteria, as appropriate.

DEALERS & SUPPLIERS DIRECTORY

ALABAMA
Michael Smith
Ditto Falls Postcards
P.O. Box 12092
Huntsville, AL 35815
205-498-3834
Postcards, Paper Collectibles

ARIZONA
Joan C. Angier
6365 W. Lost Canyon
Tucson, AZ 85745
602-743-7652
General Line

Steve Butler
2326 E. Mallard Ct.
Gilbert, AZ 85234
602-926-0456
Las Vegas, Rt. 66, Arizona

Chas. W. Heckroth
Great Western Mails
P.O. Box 31510
Tucson, AZ 85751
602-296-1432
All Countries & Types Early Postcards
    Through Linens, Mail Sales,
    Selected Approvals

Terry & Norene Pavey
Verde Paper
P.O. Box 10614
Glendale, AZ 85318
602-439-2156
Mail Approvals, Shows, Arizona

Robert C. Quay
Quay Postcards
2800 Saddleback, #4
Flagstaff, AZ 86004
Auctioneer, Broker, Dealer

Val Duane Robbins
Rimrock West
3450 North Drake Place
Tucson, AZ 85749
602-749-8774
General Line, Mail Order & By
    Appointment

Cliff Sutton
Collector's Cabinet Inc.
P.O. Box 41986
Mesa, AZ 85274-1986
602-756-0761
Real Photo Street Scenes, Rare &
    Unusual, All Topics

ARKANSAS
Tom & Sara Mertens
3605 Dunkeld Dr.
N. Little Rock, AR 72116
501-753-4254

Shows, By Appointment

CALIFORNIA
Michael Blessing
A.R.S.
24307 Majic Mtn. Pkwy., #124
Valencia, CA 91355
805-296-7586
Women, Nudes, Risque

Ralph Bowman
Paper Gallery
5349 Wheaton St.
La Mesa, CA 91942
619-462-6268
Topicals, States, Autographs, Movie
    Memorabilia

Carol Brockfield
P.O. Box 7115
Napa, CA 94558
707-224-5547
Fine & Unusual Topicals, Western Real
    Photo Views, Children's Illustrators

Lee Brown
Adventure In Postcards
8423 Foothill Blvd.
Sunland, CA 91040
818-352-5663, 818-896-7919
Postcards, Paper Ephemera, Movie
    Material

Gloria & Rudy Cazanjian
26920 Almaden Court
Los Altos Hills, CA 94022
415-941-1819
Children, Dolls, General

Gordie Chamberlin
Gordie's Used Cards
1235 Vista Superba
Glendale, CA 91205
818-246-6686
Motor Vehicle Related, Sells By Mail,
    Appointment, At Shows

Bill Colby
Kenrich Co.
9418 Las Tunas Dr.
Temple City, CA 91780
818-286-3888
Baseball Cards, Stamps, Autographs

Dorothy DeMare
Pastime Postcards
1024 Garfield Dr.
Petaluma, CA 94954-5836
707-763-9736

Alan DePauli
P.O. Box 704
Lodi, CA 95241
209-943-5016
Mail Auctions

Gisela Granstrom
4418 Dean Dr.
Ventura, CA 93003
805-642-0534
Auctions, Approvals

Bill & Marilyn Hanson
P.O. Box 901
Ben Lomond, CA 95005-0901
408-336-5001
Better Views & Topicals

Harold Holman
1212 Third St.
P.O. Box 416
Atwater, CA 95301
209-357-1373, 209-358-2671
Signed Artists, Old Postcards

Joseph C. Jaynes
P.O. Box 1155
Santa Cruz, CA 95061
408-476-3262

Roger LeRoque & Nick Farago
R & N Postcards
P.O. Box 217
Temple City, CA 91780
818-287-6066
West Coast Show Promoters

Rita Nadler
Postcards, Etc.
P.O. Box 4318
Thousand Oaks, CA 91359
805-497-1725
Topics, Tucks, Signed Artists

Vic Pallos
658 Arden Ave.
Glendale, CA 91202
818-242-9055
Baseball Stadiums

Ken Prag
Paper Americana
P.O. Box 531
Burlingame, CA 94011
415-566-6400 (San Francisco)
Quality Western State Views, Better
    Topicals, Stock Certificates & Bonds

Mike Rasmussen
Everything Paper
P.O. Box 726
Marina, CA 93933
408-384-5460
Postcards, Movie Memorabilia,
    Autographs, Appraisals, Auctions

Pete Richards
Davis Gold & Silver Exchange
330 G St., Suite H
Davis, CA 95616
916-758-1334

Pre-1940 Western States, Real Photos,
    General Topics
Steve Schmale
Out West
448 Tanglewood Court
Santa Rosa, CA 95409
707-538-8948
Western State Views, Photos, Paper;
    Railroadiana; Sports: Golf, Baseball
Carole Steele
Carole's Cards
Rt. 2, Box 218P
Willows, CA 95988
916-934-3427
Mail Approvals
Norm & Bess Sturgess
Inland Empire Postcards
360 W. 24th St.
San Bernardino, CA 92405
909-883-9075
Postcards, Advertising Cards
Harry A. Victor
1422 18th Ave.
San Francisco, CA 94122
415-664-4286
Cigarette, Food & Beverage Cards,
    Sports, Films, Transportation
COLORADO
Chuck Finley
Chuck Finley's Post Cards
302 Michigan Place
Pueblo, CO 81004
719-543-0003
Colorado, Suffrage, Circus, Billy
    Possum, Carousels
Hope Firkins-Duncan
The Paper Lady
1850 Folsom St., #209
Boulder, CO 80302
303-442-0772
States, Artist Signed, Real Photos
Ron & Carmen Schwartz
P.O. Box 440068
Aurora, CO 80044
303-750-4695
Colorado, Real Photos, Oklahoma,
    Nebraska, Approval Service,
    Buying Quality Greetings &
    Western U.S. Real Photos
CONNECTICUT
Carl Kallgren
Carl's Cards
49 Goodhouse Rd.
Litchfield, CT 06759
203-567-8091
Connecticut Views, General Collection,
    By Appointment
Russell Norton
P.O. Box 1070
New Haven, CT 06504
203-562-7800
Supplies: Clear Archival Sleeves—12
    sizes, Price List
Jose L. Rodriguez
The Cartophilians
P.O. Box 903
430 Highland Ave.
Cheshire, CT 06410
203-272-2841, 203-272-1143

Postcards, Trade Cards, U.S. Postal
    History, Paper Americana
Murray & Joanne Ruggiero
Ruggiero's
359 Silver Sands Rd.
East Haven, CT 06512-4125
203-469-7083
Worldwide Views, Topicals, Greetings,
    Postcards on Approval
Mary Ellen & Bob Seward
Sewards' Folly
296 Palmer Hill Rd.
Riverside, CT 06878
203-637-4779
Sells At Shows
Marty Shapiro
Postcards International
P.O. Box 2930
New Haven, CT 06515
203-865-0814, FAX 203-495-8005
First National Postcard Auctions, The
    Vintage Picture Postcard Catalog,
    Postcards Direct Mail Approval
    Service
DELAWARE
Neal & Tillie Boyle
1545 Savannah Rd.
Lewes, DE 19958
302-645-7604
Edward J. Masci
21 Hilton Rd.
Wilmington, DE 19810
302-475-8640
FLORIDA
Theodore E. Bachman
650 Baffin Dr. W.
Venice, FL 34293
813-497-6917
David C. Brown
7540 SW 59 Ct., Suite #3
South Miami, FL 33143
305-665-6092
Worldwide Views, Greetings, Topicals
Wm. M. & Gladys A. Bruce
Postcard Nostalgia
40 Sabal Palm Circle (Winter)
Eustis, FL 32726
904-357-9403
Small Town USA & World, All Topics
Edward M. Carter
Ed Carter - Postcards
P.O. Box 158
Boca Raton, FL 33429
Robert L. Damery
Covered Bridge Postcards & Old Mills
2000 Burma Rd.
New Smyrna Beach, FL 32168
904-428-3601
Round Barns
Coby & Hank de Boer
St. Johns Stamp Shop
2 Aviles St.
St. Augustine, FL 32084
904-829-9673
Stamps, Postcards, Baseball Cards
Enrique de la Vega
12225 SW 24 Terrace
Miami, FL 33175
305-226-8296

Cuba, Spanish American War
Ed & Millie Goheen
Edward W. Goheen
6848 Tiburon Dr.
Boca Raton, FL 33433
407-361-9201
Alan F. Grab
Grab Bag Antiques, Inc.
10836 N.W. 30th Place (Winter)
Sunrise, FL 33322
305-572-4107
Quality Postcards, Paper Ephemera,
    Prints
Bernice & Robert Kaufman
The Remember Gallery
1239 S. Tamiami Trail
Sarasota, FL 34239
813-955-2625, 813-952-1570
Small Town USA Views, Old Paper,
    Antiques
Clayton & Evelyn Keehn
Keehn Kollectibles
2117 Barcelona Dr.,
Clearwater, FL 34624
813-531-4807
Views, Sports, General Line
Audrey K. Malone
1531 N. Drexel Rd.
Lot #409
West Palm Beach, FL 33417
407-687-3378
State Views, Detroit Publishing Co.,
    Edward H. Mitchell Publisher
Ronald D. Millard
Cherryland Auctions
P.O. Box 4086
Tequesta, FL 33469
407-743-0010
Postcard Mail Auctions
Charles R. Mullin
2653 Grand Cayman St.
Sarasota, FL 34231
813-922-2246
Florida, Staten Island NY, Foxes
Marie H. Nemeth
325 S. Inglis Ave.
Inglis, FL 34449
904-447-2368
Signed Artists, Union Oil, Greetings
Larry P. Noder
P.O. Box 962
Odessa, FL 33556
813-376-5851
U.S. Military, German Military
Joan & Robert Rau
2600 SE Ocean Blvd., V-9 (Winter)
Stuart, FL 34996
407-286-5035
Hobart Smith
10813 Main St., Lot #10
Thonotosassa, FL 33592
813-896-4541
Topics, Views, Foreign, Mail Orders &
    Appointment Sales Only
Van R. Tippett
Tippett, Inc.
6625 Gateway Ave.
Sarasota, FL 34231
813-925-3772

General Line
JoAnn & Bob Van Scotter
JoAnn Van Scotter Postcards
4730 NW 10th Ct., #318 (Winter)
Plantation, FL 33313
305-583-8228
Views, Transportation, Sports
Michael B. Wasserberg
OJUS Tropical Topicals
1025 Country Club Dr.
Margate, FL 33063-3251
305-972-3789
Estate Liquidations, Buys Postcards,
	Auction Sales Only
GEORGIA
J.C. Ballentine
Ballentines
P.O. Box 761
Hatcher Point Mall
Waycross, GA 31501
912-285-3250
Billy Horne
Mallard Nest Antiques
5860 Bankston Lake Rd.
Macon, GA 31206
912-788-8606
Blacks, Georgia
Jack & Michael Leach
National Postcard Exchange
P.O. Box 886
225 Third St.
Macon, GA 31202-0886
912-743-8951
Rare Postcards, Common Postcards,
	General Line
Ernest P. Malcom
Malcom Postcards
P.O. Box 453
433 Plaza
Monroe, GA 30655
404-267-6897
General Line
Charles McCoy
Charlie's Cards
P.O. Box 516
180 Parkview Dr.
Commerce, GA 30529
706-335-3976
Buying All Cards For Resale, Send For
	Offer
Vickie & George Prater
Shiloh Postcards
P.O. Box 2004
Clayton, GA 30525
706-782-4100
Southern States, Archival Quality
	Supplies
IDAHO
Vernon Ham
Ham's Cards
945 S. 5th St.
St. Maries, ID 83861
208-245-4865
Mitchell & Newman Cards & Check-
	lists, Detroit Publishing Cards,
	Want Lists Welcome
ILLINOIS
Helen O. Ackert
Ackert Enterprises

521 S. 7th St.
DeKalb, IL 60115-3838
815-758-8236
Ackert Doll Postcards, DeKalb Area,
	Assortment of Old Postcards
Jerry Andreen
Jerry's Cards
2304 17th Ave.
Rockford, IL 61104
815-398-6380
Holger (Danny) & Kathy Danielsen
Metro-East Promotions & Postcard
	Shop
P.O. Box 1208
O'Fallon, IL 62269
618-632-1921
Views, Greetings, Shop Sales
Dunnings Auction Service, Inc.
755 Church Rd.
Elgin, IL 60123
708-741-3483
Postcards, Paper Collectibles, Auto-
	graphs
William I. Galaway
The Home Place Antiques
615 S. State St.
Belvidere, IL 61008
815-544-0577
Jennifer Henderson
Cookin' with Postcards
1610 W. Highland, Suite 23
Chicago, IL 60660
312-764-4428, FAX 312-465-1898
Old & New Recipe Postcards, Root
	Beer Postcards, Food Close-up
	Postcards, Recipe & Food-Related
	Postcard Catalog ($1.00)
Dwane Kaplenk
Rock Aires Postcards
P.O. Box 2301
Loves Park, IL 61131
815-398-0813
Street Scenes, Topicals, Advertising
John W. Kuster
Yesteryear's Paper
102 Shady Lane Dr.
Dixon, IL 61021
815-288-2163
Riverboats, Railroad, Movie Stars,
	Amusement Parks, Iowa, Illinois,
	379 Categories
Ed McAllister
3413 W. Jefferson
Joliet, IL 60435
815-725-2504
Susan Nicholson
P.O. Box 595
Lisle, IL 60532
No View Cards
Michael & Barbara Nolan
1513 Cedar Lane
Northbrook, IL 60062
708-272-1920
General Line, Patriotics, Views
Darlene & Wally Schultz
Remembered Treasures
230 N. Forest Court
Palatine, IL 60067
708-358-3226

Topicals, States, Foreign
Fred F. Solberger
13006 N. Coon
Orangeville, IL 61060
815-789-4277
Street Scenes, Depots
Rob Swanson
924 17th St.
Rockford, IL 61104
815-398-5384
JoAnn & Bob Van Scotter
JoAnn Van Scotter Postcards
208 E. Lincoln St. (Summer)
Mt. Morris, IL 61054
815-734-6971
Views, Transportation, Sports
Arretta Wetzel
1325 45 St.
Rock Island, IL 61201
309-786-1335
Topicals, Greetings
INDIANA
Michael Fallon
Hobby House Distributing
P.O. Box 18025
Indianapolis, IN 46218
317-966-6939 (info)
800-544-6229 (orders)
Supplies: Close Fit Sleeves, Catalog
	($2.00 or free with order)
Jerry & Sandi Garrett
Jerry's Antiques
1807 W. Madison St.
Kokomo, IN 46901
317-457-5256
Real Photos, Small Town Street Scenes
Dave Long & Diane Allmen
Modern Postcard Sales
P.O. Box 644
Elkhart, IN 46515
219-264-0013
Modern Topicals, Chrome Views, 1960s
	To Present
Walter E. & Phyllis E. Mitchell
Walt & Phyl's Cards
611 Park Terrace
Columbia City, IN 46725-1949
219-244-4561
Street Scenes, IFPD Member
Ernest E. Parker
Parker's Hobby Shop
P.O. Box 74
Mishawaka, IN 46544
U.S. Old Photos, Arcade Cards
Robert Pickard
M. & B. Hobbies
5010 W. 22nd St.
Indianapolis, IN 46224-5017
317-241-8777
No Approvals
Gerald Sanders
Antiques & Things
24 Fall St.
Williamsport, IN 47993
317-762-3687
Real Photos, U.S. Views, Signed Artists
Jack & Vicki Stock
Retrospection
7850 Camelback Dr.

✱ 79

Indianapolis, IN 46250
317-841-7342
Rare & Unusual, Quality Greetings,
  Topicals
Anthony C. Turner
P.O. Box 905
Goshen, IN 46526
219-534-3015
Real Photos, Roadside, Transportation
John R. Weaver
Just Post Cards
120 W. N. A St.
Gas City, IN 46933
317-674-2574, 317-664-9467
Photo Cards, Santas, General Line
Barry & Carolyn Yancey
Barry's Postcards
P.O. Box 1865
Anderson, IN 46011
317-643-8455
Thomas M. Zollinger
1023 Markle Ave.
Elkhart, IN 46517-1620
219-522-3954
Old Cards, Moderns, Supplies

IOWA
Dr. J. W. Carberry
A&A Coins Collectables Antiques
Box 2231
Iowa City, IA 52240
319-337-9203
All Areas, Appointments & Shows
  Only
Howard Dreasler
Hamilton House Antiques
209 S. 12th St.
Fort Dodge, IA 50501
515-576-2881
Mail Auctions, Approvals
R. D. Kisch
Box 281
311 1st Ave. N.E.
West Bend, IA 50597
515-887-5072
General Line
Dean Petersen
Dean Petersen Post Cards
4232 Orleans Ave.
Sioux City, IA 51106
712-276-4760, 712-252-1060
General Line
Lois Pietz
Past & Present
435 24th St.
Ames, IA 50010
515-233-1513
Midwest Views, Artist Signed,
  Magazines
Pat & Lois Ryan
Ryan's Cards
343 26th St. N.W.
Cedar Rapids, IA 52405
319-396-7241
Depots, Topicals, Towns
Wally & Charlene Searcy
Iowa Postcard Depot
3244 Whittier Rd.
Springville, IA 52336
319-854-7359

States—Esp. Midwest, Topics—Incl.
  Photos
Herb & Mary Staub
Staub's Postcard & Paper Auctions
P.O. Box 5233
Coralville, IA 52241
319-351-3848
Old Postcards, Paper Ephemera,
  Advertising

KANSAS
Eileen & Leland Keller
Treasure Village Antiques
212 S. Broadway
Pittsburg, KS 66762
316-231-4888
Large Variety of Topics
Dick & Sue Lightle
P.O. Box 2562
Kansas City, KS 66110
913-334-3186
Hal Ottaway
Auction Americana
P.O. Box 780282
Wichita, KS 67278-0282
316-686-5574
Kansas & Bordering States, Presidential
  Campaigns, Rare & Unusual

KENTUCKY
Stan & Frances Walter
1027 Jefferson St.
Paducah, KY 42001
502-442-1740
Views Worldwide, Topics, IFPD
  Member

LOUISIANA
Rai Lynne Jarabica
Sanchez's Daughter
P.O. Box 626
Mandeville, LA 70470
504-624-9596
Always Buying, Mail Order,
  Appointments, Shows

MAINE
Pete Bosse
Pete's Cards
18 Orleans St.
Lewiston, ME 04240
207-786-3418
Real Photo Train Stations
Alan F. Grab
Grab Bag Antiques, Inc.
39 Main St. (Summer)
Sabattus, ME 04280
207-375-4711
Quality Postcards, Paper Ephemera,
  Prints
Bruce D. Nelson
Landmark Postcards
P.O. Box 3565
Portland, ME 04104
207-799-7890
Real Photos, Illustrated Government
  Postals, Pioneer, Rare & Unusual
Robert & Myra Siegel
The Salty Professor
4-1/2 Milk St.
Portland, ME 04101
207-772-4640
Postcards, Ephemera, Antiques

John Vierra
P.O. Box 6783
Portland, ME 04101
207-657-4399
Mail Order, Show Sales

MARYLAND
Al Abend
P.O. Box 421
Millington, MD 21651
301-778-1722
Stu Bramble
Stu Bramble's Postcards
523 Evergreen Rd.
Severna Park, MD 21146
410-544-5546
Buying & Selling Postcards
John Corliss
Previously Owned Postcards
P.O. Box 20899
Baltimore, MD 21209
410-235-6612
Royalty, Military, Maryland
Lee & Shirley Cox
Memory Lane Postcards, Inc.
P.O. Box 66
Keymar, MD 21757
410-775-0188
Shop Sales, Approvals, Auction, Shows
Roy Cox
P.O. Box 3610
Baltimore, MD 21214
301-483-4778
Book-"How To Price Old Picture
  Postcards"
Catalog-"1992 Specialized Picture
  Postcard Catalog"
Eden Delcher & B.J. Francis
Emerald Aisle Postcards & Ephemera
413 E. Lake Ave.
Baltimore, MD 21212
410-433-1532
Fantasy, Holidays, Flowers
Sheldon Dobres
S. Dobres
P.O. Box 1855
Baltimore, MD 21203-1855
410-486-6569 (eve)
Moderns, Better Pre-1920
Perry Judelson
P.O. Box 7675
Baltimore, MD 21207
410-655-5239
Views, Topicals, Comprehensive Stock,
  Shows, No Mail Order
Fred H. Lego
6506 Kipling Parkway
Forestville, MD 20747
301-735-6556
By Mail & Appointment Only
Mary L. Martin
Mary L. Martin LTD.
4899 Pulaski Hwy.
Perryville, MD 21903
301-575-7768, 301-642-3521
Topicals, U.S. Views, Supplies,
  Approvals
Lee Moore
101 Seminole Ave.
Catonsville, MD 21228

301-747-8521
States, Holidays, Foreign
Fava C. Sherrard
Fava Cards
455 Spring Hill Rd.
Rising Sun, MD 21911
410-658-6359
Donald E. Wachter
923 Seminole Rd.
Frederick, MD 21701
301-662-1258

MASSACHUSETTS
Paul & Sandra Anna
Anna's Postcards & Collectables
127 Gaslight Dr., #3
South Weymouth, MA 02190
617-331-9850
Views, Topicals
Bill Cole Enterprises, Inc.
P.O. Box 60
Randolph, MA 02368-0060
617-986-2653, FAX 617-986-2656
Archival Supplies: Mylar Sleeves,
    Catalog
H.J.W. Daugherty
Philatelic Auctions
P.O. Box 1146
Eastham, MA 02642
508-255-7488
Auctions
Stan Davidson
The Post Card Stand
P.O. Box 872
West Yarmouth, MA 02673
508-771-5435
S/A Comics, Vinelines, Dwigs
Siegfried Feller
Cartomania Plus
8 Amherst Rd.
Pelham, MA 01002
413-253-3115
Postcards By Topic & Place
    (Esp. Germany & France), Maps,
    Ephemera
Howard D. Goodwin
18 Willard St.
Wareham, MA 02571-1241
508-295-5857
New England Views & Railroad
    Depots, B&W Photo Postcards
Harris & Jayne Gray
The Grays
P.O. Box 246
Brookfield, MA 01506
508-867-7210
U.S. Views, Topicals, Postcard Supplies
Tom Holland
Falmouth Stamp & Coin
11 Town Hall Square
Falmouth, MA 02540
508-548-7075
Alan R. Lavendier
Whale Deltiology
P.O. Box 40812
New Bedford, MA 02744
508-993-9006
Theodore Roosevelt, World's Fairs,
    New Bedford, MA
Walter E. Lenk

Walter's Memorabilia
205 Brick Hill Rd.
Orleans, MA 02653
508-255-1817
New England Cards Only, Topicals
Joan G. Noble
The Quarter Deck
P.O. Box 75
206 Front St.
Scituate Harbor, MA 02066
617-545-4303
Scituate, South Shore of Massachusetts
Michael O'Brien
309 Reservoir St.
N. Attleboro, MA 02760
508-695-8158
Mail Auctions
Art Ross
P.O. Box 95
Dennis, MA 02638
508-385-5480
Dick & Marie Soffey
House on the Hill Antiques
17 Seaview St.
Chatham, MA 02633
508-945-2290
Postcards, Political Items, Baseball
    Cards, Advertising Items
Richard Spedding
Richard's Postcards
22 Tanglewood Rd.
Sterling, MA 01564
508-422-8480
Topicals, Views, Approvals
Edward F. Stefanik
P.O. Box 2558
Fall River, MA 02722
508-674-9090
MA & RI Postcards, Sportscards,
    Autographs
Mary C. Valentine
115 Willow St.
New Bedford, MA 02740-4557
Lighthouses, Views
Ed Valladoa
Valladoa's
P.O. Box 484
84 Rt. 6
Mattapoisett, MA 02739
508-758-3381
Shop Sales Only (10-4), Pleasant Prices,
    Topicals, U.S. Views, World-Wide
    Selection, Collector's Plates, Paper
Gregory Wilson
Buttons By Wilson
215 Chestnut St.
Florence, MA 01060
413-586-8554
Show Advertising Products, Buttons,
    Award Ribbons, Stickers, Catalog

MICHIGAN
Matt Abbott
Abbott's Coinex
1393 S. Woodward Ave.
Birmingham, MI 48009
313-642-5081, FAX 313-644-7038
Don Hatfield
Box 347
Fowlerville, MI 48836

517-223-7575
Small Michigan Town Main Streets
David Jaeger
Dave's New & Used Cards
9114 Warner Rd.
Haslett, MI 48840
517-675-5474
Real Photos, Views, Misc. Paper
Laurence & Elizabeth Nordhoff
Trade Winds
336 N. Main St.
P.O. Box 248
Watervliet, MI 49098
616-463-8281
Michigan Views, House of David
Michael G. Price
M.G. Price
P.O. Box 7071
Ann Arbor, MI 48107
313-668-7388
Foreign Countries, Mail Order
Judy Ripple
1038 S. Main St., Apt. F2
Ann Arbor, MI 48104
313-994-5739, 313-764-3167
Pre-1920 Greetings & Topicals
Doris Waggoner & Kathi Gorske
Postcards from the Attic & Cellar
P.O. Box 145
Williamsburg, MI 49690
616-267-5506
Martha J. Walton
Postcard Enterprises
707 Collegewood Dr.
Ypsilanti, MI 48197
313-482-8354
Sells By Appointment & Approvals By
    Mail, Book: *Postcard Collecting, A
    Fun Investment* by the late Bernard
    Stadtmiller
Juanita E. White
55 Greble St.
Battle Creek, MI 49017
616-965-0545
Sells By Appointment
Craig Whitford
Numismatic Card Co.
P.O. Box 14255
Lansing, MI 48901
517-394-4443
Coin Cards, Macerated Cards, U.S.
    Mints

MINNESOTA
Fred & Gail Schiffman
Crossroads Stamp Shop
2211 West 54th St.
Minneapolis, MN 55419
612-928-0119
Shop with 100,000 Postcards, M-F 11-5,
    Sa 10-4 (Win) 10-2 (Sum)
Mary Twyce
601 E. 5th St.
Winona, MN 55987
507-454-4412

MISSISSIPPI
Pat & Mike Hutter
Spanish Trail Books
1006 Thorn Ave.
Ocean Springs, MS 39564

601-875-1144
General Line, Shop, Always Buying
Edgar & Georgia Manuel
E&G Postcards
2800 Edgewood Dr.
Meridian, MS 39307-4041
601-483-9658
U.S. States, Greetings, Trains, Indians

MISSOURI
William W. Burt
5419 Oak
Kansas City, MO 64112
816-444-5414
Ron Clark
5828 Marion Ave.
Kansas City, MO 64133
816-737-2024
State Views, Real Photos, Some
    Topicals
Stan & Jane Pepper
Pepper's Post Card Auction
3048 Dodridge Ave.
Maryland Hgts., MO 63043
314-291-5972
Auction, Approvals, Buying
Ed Robertson
Robertson's Collector's Corner
On the Square—North Side
Butler, MO 64730-2019
816-679-3971
General Line of 100,000 Cards
Pat & Pam Seeley
Postcard Collectors Unltd.
411 E. Walker
Ash Grove, MO 65604
417-672-2205

MONTANA
Jack & Susan Davis
Olde America Antiques
501 E. Peach
Bozeman, MT 59715
406-587-0937, FAX 406-587-3419
Views, Topics, Greetings, Supplies
Frank Houde
Houde's Post Cards
Box 2577
Missoula, MT 59806
406-549-2115
Approvals
Tom Mulvaney
Box 814
East Helena, MT 59635
406-227-8790
Postcards, Postal History, Photos

NEBRASKA
Bill Cloran
Abraham's Corner
2708 Y St.
Lincoln, NE 68503
402-474-2696
States, Greetings, Real Photos
Robert D. Farley
The Paper Parson
Box 34651
Omaha, NE 68134
402-571-7811
Real Photos, Paper Ephemera
John & Lynne Farr
P.O. Box 6086

Omaha, NE 68106
402-334-0284
RMS Titanic, Better Topicals,
    Midwestern States
Holmes Publishing
P.O. Box 11
Gothenburg, NE 69138
308-537-3335
Willard Mullin Postcards

NEVADA
Tracy Garrett
P.O. Box 18000-52
Las Vegas, NV 89114
702-737-3218
Approvals: Views & Topicals
Trilby Mary Roman
2304 Columbia Way
Carson City, NV 89706
702-882-0664
Western U.S. Occupations, Small
    Towns, Buy & Sell

NEW HAMPSHIRE
Michael Bennett
Michael Bennett Auctions
RFD #3, Pickering Rd.
Dover, NH 03820
800-MB-GAVEL
Auction House For High Quality
    Postcards, Large Collections &
    Individual, Rare & Unusual
Dave Bowers
P.O. Box 1224
Wolfeboro, NH 03894
603-569-5095 (weekdays)
Buying Only, Pre-1915 Real Photos Of
    New Hampshire, Motion Picture
    Theatres, Coin-operated Pianos &
    Music Boxes
Alf E. Jacobson
Burpee Hill Books
P.O. Box 188
New London, NH 03257
603-526-6654
State Views, Foreign, Holidays
James B. Kahn, MD
121 Raymond Rd., Rt. 107
Deerfield, NH 03037-1599
603-463-7105
WWII Propaganda (Germany, Italy,
    Other)
Keyle Mabin
North Country Stamps
P.O. Box 95
64 Main St.
Plymouth, NH 03264
603-536-2155, 603-536-2625
William J. Pieterse
62 Boston Post Rd.
Amherst, NH 03031
603-673-1945
Gordon Root
RFD 1 Box 93
Lancaster, NH 03584
603-788-2276
**Chris Russell & Pamela Apkarian-
    Russell**
Chris Russell & the Halloween Queen
P.O. Box 499
4 Lawrence St.

Winchester, NH 03470
603-239-8875
Halloween, Foreign Views, Posters &
    Propaganda
Dave & Brenda Trench
Western Mountain Stamp & Coin Shop
RFD #1, Box #4
Main St.
Warner, NH 03278
603-456-2141
New England Towns, Military

NEW JERSEY
Carlton F. Bloodgood
Carlton's Modern Postcards
P.O. Box 111
Bogota, NJ 07603
Classico, American, Ludlow, Dover
Saul & Marcia Bolotsky
The Paper Works
63 Columbus Ave.
Lakewood, NJ 08701-3052
908-363-2192
Lakewood, New Jersey
Barbara J. Booz
The Card Shark
1 Lewis St.
Perth Amboy, NJ 08861
908-442-4234
Northeastern State Views
Paul Brenner
Blackstamps
P.O. Box 402
South Orange, NJ 07079
201-761-0341
Blacks, Pictorial Cancellations,
    Supplies: Storage Boxes
Shirley Carroll
9 Wagner Lane
Manasquan, NJ 08736
908-223-2276
Frank Chmiel
350 Marc Dr.
Toms River, NJ 08753
908-349-5223
State Views, Patriotic, Holidays
Daniel B. Duffy
20 Lenox Ave.
Yardville, NJ 08620
609-585-6177
Sheldon Halper
Cobweb Collectibles
9 Walnut Ave.
Cranford, NJ 07016
908-272-5777
Postcards, Automobile, Toys
Eleanor & Don Hart
El-Donal Post Cards
41 Preston Ave.
Bridgeton, NJ 08302
609-451-0087
Fred Herrigel
Box 80R
Oakhurst, NJ 07755
908-775-8997
Pre-1920 Real Photos, Main Streets,
    Store Fronts
Daniel Herzog
Daniel Herzog/Mr. Postcard
P.O. Box 545

Vauxhall, NJ 07088
201-399-7717
Topicals, State Views, Foreign Cancels

John J. Kowalak
Camera Retrospect
19 Coles Ct.
Riveredge, NJ 07661
201-487-5721
Custom Real Photos, Sells At Shows,
    Buying Camera/Photography
    Cards

John McGrath
Jersey Shore Shows
95 Newbury Rd.
Howell, NJ 07731
908-363-3121
New Jersey

Vin Minner
21 Boulevard Rd.
Cedar Knolls, NJ 07927
201-267-3132
Pre-1950 Topicals & Views, Cigarette &
    Gum Cards

Richard & Anita Novick
Richard Novick Products (Card-Gard)
17 Abbey Lane
Marlboro, NJ 07746
908-536-2532
Postcards, Stamps, Supplies: Vinyl
    Pages, Binders, Polybags, Sleeves,
    Catalog (SASE)

Steve O'Conor
The Bag Man
P.O. Box 129
Vernon, NJ 07462-0129
201-764-3535
Supplies: Polysleeves, 25% Rag
    Envelopes, Catalog

Don & Newly Preziosi
Preziosi Postcards
P.O. Box 498
Mendham, NJ 07945
201-543-4721
Better Eclectic Older Cards, Top-Notch
    Linens, Contemporary Social/
    Political Issues

John F. Rhody
686 River Rd.
Fair Haven, NJ 07704
201-758-9436
Eastern State Views

Herbert & Christine Richardson
Richardson Books
209 Stratford Ave.
Westmont, NJ 08108
609-854-3348
New England & New Jersey Views,
    Farm Buildings, Mills

Pam Vlerebome
P.O. Box 190
45 Wells Ave.
Hampton, NJ 08827
908-537-2058

Donald W. Wayne
23 Plymouth Court
Piscataway, NJ 08854
201-463-1527

NEW YORK
Avis Post Card Co.

P.O. Box 14974
Albany, NY 12212-4974
Hold-to-Lights, Christmas Chromes

Edward J. Beiderbecke
P.O. Box 155
4674 Ridge Rd.
Williamson, NY 14589
315-589-2287
Real Photos, New York State Views,
    Railroad Stations

Thomas J. Boyd
140 Andover Lane
Williamsville, NY 14221
716-626-0089
State Views, World's Fairs, Santas,
    Halloween

Ken Butts
The Picture Post Card Man
97 Fairhaven Dr.
Cheektowaga, NY 14225
716-634-5970
New York State, Elvis, Trains,
    Airplanes

Agnes Cavalari
Old Windsor Antiques
R.D. #2, 345 Bethlehem Rd.
New Windsor, NY 12553
914-564-6775
Northeastern States, Glamour

Frank & Hilda Ely
P.O. Box 129
19 North St.
Livonia, NY 14487
716-346-3715

Armando J. Florez
16 Park Ave.
New York, NY 10016
212-889-4767
Cuba, Spain, Latin America, All
    Categories, Rare Early Postcards,
    Real Photos

Nancy Foutz
2182 Lucas Tpke.
High Falls, NY 12440
914-687-0175
Real Photos, Advertising &
    Government Postals, Shows, Mail
    Order

George C. Gibbs
601 New Loudon Rd., #219
Latham, NY 12110
518-786-3292
Postcard Auctions Specializing In
    Transportation, Greetings, Political,
    Artist, Real Photo & Better
    Miscellaneous Topics

Marilyn Gottlieb
Marilyn's House of Postcards
P.O. Box 35
Rock Hill, NY 12775
914-796-3244
U.S. Small Towns, Foreign, Topicals

John & Betty Henel
79 Fruehauf Ave.
Snyder, NY 14226
716-839-4174
Views, Entertainers, Ships

Charlie & Nellie Huttunen
9 Birmingham Dr.

Northport, NY 11768
516-261-4031
Long Island, New York, New England

Mike Jacobs & Nadine Kagan
Matrix Gallery
11 Flower Rd.
Valley Stream, NY 11581
516-791-8251
Native American Indians, Military,
    Monkeys/Chimps

Robert E. Juceam
Philatelic Specialties Co.
106 Hemlock Rd.
Manhasset, NY 11030
516-365-7696, FAX 516-365-7697
Stamp Cards, Third Reich Propaganda
    Cards

Joan & Jeff Kay
1816 E. 26th St.
Brooklyn, NY 11229
718-375-7353
5 New York City Boroughs, Long
    Island, Advertising, New Jersey

Bob & Mary Kurey
The Post Card People
585 Overbrook Rd.
Johnson City, NY 13790
607-797-3040
Photo Cards

S.R. Nelms
P.O. Box 633
Hicksville, NY 11756
516-579-9432
General Postcard Line

Vincent Peterson, Jr.
928 Dellapenna Dr.
Johnson City, NY 13790
85 Catagories

Frank J. Pichardo
P.O. Box 1116
Flushing, NY 11354-0035
718-359-1183
World Ocean Liners, Ship
    Cancellations, Cuba, Puerto Rico,
    General Line

Joan & Robert Rau
Trackside 2, C-11 (Summer)
Johnstown, NY 12095
518-736-1163

Leah Schnall
67-00 192nd St.
Flushing, NY 11365
718-454-1272, 718-454-0582

Jane Schryver
226 Main St.
Dansville, NY 14437
716-335-3121
Views

Robert Skotarski
Bare Jays Air
35 Cardy Lane
Depew, NY 14043
716-683-2322
Commercial Airplanes, Airports

Tom & Pat Snyder
PSC 2
Box 9447
APO, AE 09012

Fred Timan

Atlantis Rising
545 Warren St.
Hudson, NY 12534
518-822-0438
Postcards, Paper Ephemera
Barbara H. Trovei
Barbara's PaperTiques
P.O. Box 317
Port Jervis, NY 12771
914-856-8572
Postcards, Books, Paper Collectibles
Todd & Constance Weseloh
The Anglophile Owl & The Yankee
    Frog
506 Dewitt St.
Syracuse, NY 13203
315-479-9032
American Canals, Real Photo Views,
    Central New York
Nancy Williams
Nancy's Antiques
7217 Lake Ave.
Williamson, NY 14589
315-589-8400
Pre-1920 Postcards, Advertising Trade
    Cards, Trade Catalogs
Florence (Flo) Wit
Flo's Follies
120 Paumanake Ave.
Babylon, NY 11702-1912
516-661-0522, FAX 516-422-3655
Rock & Roll, Pin-Ups, Postcard Related
NORTH CAROLINA
Thomas O. Dekle
The Dekles
2640 Cannon Farm Rd.
China Grove, NC 28023
704-932-8511
Early Town Views, Hold-to-Lights,
    Signed Artists
Fred N. Kahn
258 Stratford Rd.
Asheville, NC 28804
704-252-6507
U.S. Views, Topicals
Joe L. Mashburn
Mashburn Cards-Colonial House
P.O. Box 609
Enka, NC 28728
704-667-1427
Artist Signed
Herbert & Norma Schulman
Another World
P.O. Box 507
Haywood Rd.
Dillsboro, NC 28725
704-586-6572
Antique Postcards, Sports Cards,
    Antique Photographs, Stamp
    Collecting, Multi-Hobby Supplies
OHIO
Sam Armao
35887 Mildred St.
N. Ridgeville, OH 44039
216-327-1098
No Mail Sales
Kenneth P. Brady
The Paper Chasers
3381 W. 130th St.

Cleveland, OH 44111
216-941-9127
Postcards, Catalogs, Children's Books
Nancy Buckalew
Victorian Parlour Postcards
7340 Case Rd.
N. Ridgeville, OH 44039
216-327-0041
Holidays, Cats, Artist Signed
Ellen H. Budd
6910 Tenderfoot Lane
Cincinnati, OH 45249
513-489-0518
Signed Artists, Topicals, Clapsaddle &
    Brundage Books, Approvals, No
    City/Town Views
Michael Collins
Box 229
Bryan, OH 43506
Midwest Views, Real Photos
Mike Gray
5911 Ashcroft Dr.
Mayfield Hts., OH 44124
216-449-8684
Liebig's Extract Trade Cards, Old U.S.
    Cigarette Cards
Rose Mary Green
2864 Hastings Rd.
Cuyahoga Falls, OH 44224-3754
216-923-9362
Postcards, Trade Cards, Ephemera
Clay Griffin
1100 Merriman Rd.
Akron, OH 44303
216-867-7290
Russell E. Hartzell
Gene's Cards
2300 Glenway Rd.
Dayton, OH 45404
513-233-6921
Linens, Older Cards
George & Dolores Hrdlicka
G & D Collectibles
97 Firebush Lane
Northfield Center, OH 44067
216-467-7698
World War II Military, Santa Catalina
    California
Paul W. Jones
217 N. Prospect St.
Bowling Green, OH 43402
419-352-8657
Ohio, Folders, British Movie Stars
Keith B. Knight
Mail Pouch Antiques
311 Cass St.
Maumee, OH 43537
419-893-2708
Real Photos, Ohio & Michigan, Great
    Lakes Ships, Signed Artists
Karl Korzeniewski
249 East Baird Ave.
Barberton, OH 44203
216-745-7703
Jo Long
1437 Mayland Dr.
Cincinnati, OH 45230-2753
513-231-9289
Topicals, Coral-Lee

Thomas M. Major
MAJORSTAMPS
P.O. Box 808
Columbus, OH 43216
TEL/FAX 614-875-7003
Postcards, U.S. Stamps & Coins,
    Covers, Supplies: Storage Boxes,
    Polysleeves
John & Sandy Millns
Millns Postcards
40 N. Third St.
Waterville, OH 43566
419-878-0285
Quality Cards, Mail Approvals, No
    Views
Betty Powell
P.O. Box 571
Worthington, OH 43085
Artist Signed, Topicals, Views
Elliot & Ann Robins
Xenia Antiques
P.O. Box 615
Xenia, OH 45385
513-376-8065
Don Skillman
Skillman's Postcards
6646 Shiloh Rd.
Goshen, OH 45122
513-625-9518
C.R. Smith
88 Maureen Dr.
Heath, OH 43056
614-522-3075
Ohio Views, Pool/Billiards
E. K. Springston
1610 Park Ave., W.
Mansfield, OH 44906
419-529-3667
General Line
Tracy Terek
Teaticket Auctions
439 Crossbrook Dr.
Berea, OH 44017
216-826-1954
Auctions, Topical Approvals
Jeannine M. Traner
Christopher's
15267 Forest Park Dr.
Strongsville, OH 44136-3632
216-572-4932
Auctions, Mail Approvals, Shows
OKLAHOMA
John & Jean Dunning
J & J Junk
P.O. Box 14033
Oklahoma City, OK 73113
405-840-4035
Buy, Sell, Trade
Letha Martin
The Martin House
3216 E. Haskell
Tulsa, OK 74110-5534
918-834-2783
All Categories, Indians, Blacks,
    Railroad Stations, Holidays
OREGON
Michael A. Cotta
Rogue Valley Coin Exchange
41 S. Grape

Medford, OR 97501
503-772-2766
Western States
Maxine Cozzetto
Maxine Cozzetto Antiques
2228 N.E. Glisan
Portland, OR 97232
503-232-4656
Most Catagories, Buys Collections
Jocelyn Howells & Edouard Pecourt
Jocelyn Postcards
P.O. Box 22223
Portland, OR 97269
503-658-6437
Quality Cards—All Kinds, Sells By
    Appointment, Shows
Alisa Peterson
Peterson's Postcards
1531 SW Montgomery
Portland, OR 97201
503-228-4687, 503-274-2858
Mail Auctions, Antique Shows, No
    Views
Doug Walberg
Glimpse of Time
Route 1, Box 428
Bandon, OR 97411
503-347-3881
Real Photos, Photographs
Shirley M. Wilson & Harry M. Kelsey
Rainbow's End Book Co.
250 Broadalbin St. S.W.
Albany, OR 97321
503-926-3867
Pre-1920 Oregon & Washington,
    General Line, No Mail Approvals

PENNSYLVANIA
Wayne F. Bailey
Treasure Chest
P.O. Box 187
Rt. 15
Covington, PA 16917
717-659-5413
No Mail Order, Shop Only
Henry & Rowena Betz
HRB Collectibles
Fayetteville Antique Mall
Fayetteville, PA 17201
717-263-3165
General Line
Norm & Barry Brauer
Norm & Barry Brauer Post Cards
114 West Main St.
Dalton, PA 18414-0424
717-563-2244
Local Small Town Views, Specialty
    Advertising
Wm. M. & Gladys A. Bruce
Postcard Nostalgia
70 Snyders Lane, Box 23 (Summer)
Ephrata, PA 17522
717-733-0757
Small Town USA & World, All Topicals
Elaine Buck-Levin
Elaine's Postcards & Ephemera
5250 Simpson Ferry Rd., Suite 342
Mechanicsburg, PA 17055
717-697-0185
PA Views, Topics, Greetings, Trade

Cards
Anne A. Darrah
Merritts Museum of Childhood
R.D. #2, Route 422
Douglassville, PA 19518
215-385-3408
Postcards, Paper Ephemera, Gifts
Jon & Sherri Edelman
Edelman's
301 Old York Rd.
Jenkintown, PA 19046
215-572-6480
U.S. & W.W., Retail Store
Doris Kay Feight
806 Stanley Ave.
Chambersburg, PA 17201
717-263-1638
Sells By Appointment, Shows
Leo & Helma Frantz
588 Old York Rd.
Etters, PA 17319
717-938-2776
Jere H. Greider
3724 Kennel Ave.
Columbia, PA 17512
717-285-5872
Topicals, Views, Ephemera, Approvals
C. Roy Hall
Hall's Collectables
P.O. Box 33
1 Wilson Ave.
Susquehanna, PA 18847
717-853-3200
Views, Photocards, Stereo View Cards,
    Milk Creamers
Emily & Hawk Jamieson
Jamieson's Post Cards & Antiques
P.O. Box 537
I-80 at Rt. 18
Mentzers Antique Market
West Middlesex, PA 16159
216-545-3963, 412-528-2300
Pennsylvania & Ohio, Topics, State &
    Foreign-180,000 In Stock
Britt & Pamela Johnson
Johnson's Postcards
602R Baldwin St.
Bridgeville, PA 15017-2525
412-221-8466, FAX 412-221-7789
Auction House, Retail Collectibles Shop
John W. Klein
Klein's Postcards
P.O. Box 1363
West Chester, PA 19380
Real Photos, Topicals, Views
Walter T. Koch
4 E. Langborne Ave.
Havertown, PA 19083
215-446-2746
James Luty
110 Locust Way
Dillsburg, PA 17019
717-432-2619
Pennsylvania
Jay Miller
725 S. Schell St.
Philadelphia, PA 19147
215-925-3839
Advertising, Fab 50's, Unusual Photos,

Mid-Atlantic Views
Regis H. Nale
R.D. #2, Box 1065
Claysburg, PA 16625
814-239-2024
Mail Sales, Shows, Appointment
Gary Radtke
11415 Green Ridge Dr.
Waynesboro, PA 17268
Mail Order, Approvals
Dolores I. Rowe
Collectors' Rowe
123 Magnolia St.
Kennett Square, PA 19348
215-444-0641
Views, Chester County Pennsylvania,
    Hawaii
Dede & Daisy Schaeffer
Dede Schaeffer
415 Spencer Ave.
Lancaster, PA 17603
717-392-3955
Choice Catagories, No Views
Bob & Kay Schies
Bob & Kay Schies Postcards
452 E. Bissell Ave.
Oil City, PA 16301
814-677-3182
Buy & Sell Pre-1920 Postcards
Robert H. Shaub
350 W. Railroad Ave.
Shrewsbury, PA 17361
717-235-3309
Alan E. Stricker
The Nickel Trader
3025 Washington Rd.
McMurray, PA 15317
412-941-2338
Fulltime Shop, Approvals, Shows
George Trach
Box 67
Rillton, PA 15678
412-446-7627
PA & State Views, Misc. Categories
Jim Ward
P.O. Box 300
Lititz, PA 17543-0300
717-626-4660
Lancaster City & County, Pretzels On
    Postcards, Buying Postcard
    Reference Books
Evan & Fran Zlock
Newtown Coin & Collectibles
129 N. State St.
Newtown, PA 18940
215-968-7650

TENNESSEE
Paul E. Garland
1919 Rosemont Circle
Louisville, TN 37777
615-970-3271
Tennessee, Southern States, Utah

TEXAS
Agnes Barnes
3533 Basque
Waco, TX 76710
817-776-1783
1950-1970 Chromes, Real Photos
    (France, Mexico)

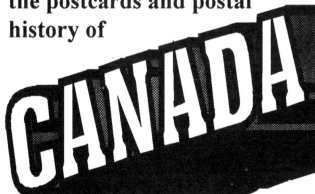

Glenn J. Butler
P.O. Box 28757
Dallas, TX 75228
214-327-0626
Texas, Transportation, Better Cards
H.D. Conner
Hal Conner Postcards
1604 Blue Bonnet Dr.
Fort Worth, TX 76111-1513
817-838-5000
Railroad Depot Real Photos
David Crockett
3215 Memphis
Nederland, TX 77627
409-727-4402
State Views, Topicals, Texas
James Dehne
Lakeshore Numismatics
Rt. 2, Box 445-B
Wills Point, TX 75169
903-560-1522
Buying, Selling, Auctioning Real Photo
   Postcards
Irmabeth Dittmer
Penny's Postcards
619 Thistlewood Dr.
Houston, TX 77079
713-497-4780
Bob & Kathy Fesler
Fesler's Auctions
Box 202284
Austin, TX 78720
Mail Auctions, Buying Collections
Laurence Gretsky
1507 Edgewood Ave.
Austin, TX 78722
512-476-7063
General Topics, Aviation/Space, Texas
Devon Hart
8502 Woodcamp
Houston, TX 77088
713-999-3936
Dwight M. March
Dwight March Enterprises
3740 Pageant Place
Dallas, TX 75244-7031
214-243-5767
Wholesale (To The Public) Supplies:
   Postcard, Stamp, Baseball Card,
   Coin, Catalog
William & Patricia Petersen
322 Scott St.
San Marcos, TX 78666
512-353-7574
Ruth Scott
1615 Bluebonnet Dr.
Fort Worth, TX 76111
817-834-0103
General Line
Jack & Billie Thornhill
833 Magnolia
Garland, TX 75040
214-276-3089, 800-638-6784
General Line, Shows, By Appointment
UTAH
Dennis B. Goreham
Goreham Collectibles
1539 East, 4070 South
Salt Lake City, UT 84124

801-277-5119
Better Topicals, Shows, Approvals
VERMONT
Jack Hamelle
Shepard's Pie in the Sky
50 Canada St.
Swanton, VT 05488
802-868-2264
Topicals, Vermont
John Larson
P. O. Box 3,
Main St.
Fairlee, VT 05045
802-333-4784
Vermont Views, General Line
VIRGINIA
Jeff Bradfield
Jeff's Antiques
745 Hillview Dr.
Dayton, VA 22821
703-879-9961
Rocky's Antique Mall
Rt. 11
Weyers Cave, VA
703-234-9900
Virginia Views, General State Views &
   Topics
Conservation Resources International
8000-H Forbes Place
Springfield, VA 22151
800-634-6932
Archival Supplies, Catalog
Charles W. Evans
118 Brown Bark Pl.
Ashland, VA 23005
804-798-0534
Baseball Postcards
Gayle Floyd
8107 Greeley Blvd.
Springfield, VA 22152
703-569-9566
Early Washington D.C., Greeting Cards,
   Hand-Colored French Romantic
   (WWI Era)
Dr. & Mrs. Bob Gardner
Dr. Nostalgia
3237 Downing Dr.
Lynchburg, VA 24503
Shows Only: Topicals, State Views,
   Foreign
Matt Godek
Rugby & Soccer Supply
P.O. Box 565
Merrifield, VA 22116
703-280-5540
Rugby & Soccer
Bob Karrer
P.O. Box 6094
Alexandria, VA 22306
703-360-5105
Panama Canal Zone, Rep. of Panama
John H. McClintock
Postcard Society, Inc.
P.O. Box 1765
Manassas, VA 22110
703-368-2757
Show Promoter, Mail Auctions
Mary Jayne Rowe
Mary Jayne's Railroad Specialties, Inc.

1905 Dressler Dr.
Covington, VA 24426
703-962-6698
Publishes & Imports Transportation
   Related Postcards
WASHINGTON
Mike Fairley
Fairlook Antiques
81-1/2 S. Washington
Seattle, WA 98104
206-622-5130, 206-364-9997
Postcards, Photos, Ephemera
Joan Klepac
The Ultimate Pet
28828 207th Ave. S.E.
Kent, WA 98042
206-630-2012
Dogs, Horses, Approvals
Michael Maslan
Michael Maslan Historic Photos,
   Postcards & Ephemera
P.O. Box 20639
1216 3rd Ave.
Seattle, WA 98102
206-587-0187
Real Photos, Ephemera, Photographs
Richard & Myra McDonald
R&M International
P.O. Box 6278
Bellevue, WA 98008-0278
206-865-8104
Auctions, Shows, Approvals
John F. McNamara
Columbia View Cards
Box 512
Long Beach, WA 98631
206-642-3398
Covered Bridges, Trains, Airplanes
Burton E. Pendleton Sr.
Vintage Postcards
E. 2130 Sprague Ave.
Spokane, WA 99202
509-535-4368
Pre-1930, Photographica
Kent & Sandra Renshaw
Potlatch Traders
P.O. Box 574
Freeland, WA 98249
206-331-0729
High Quality Subject Cards & Real
   Photos, Victorian Ephemera
Virgil Reynolds
P.O. Box 194
Walla Walla, WA 99362
509-525-6410
Topicals, States
Robert Ward
Antique Paper Guild
P.O. Box 5742
Bellevue, WA 98006
206-643-5701
Mail Auctions for Pre-1935 Real Photos
WEST VIRGINIA
Richard Bain
P.O. Box 2
Colliers, WV 26035
304-527-1724
Mail Only
Curtis & Ruth Duckett

P.O. Box 674
Rainelle, WV 25962-0674
304-438-7659
Pre-1920 & Real Photo State Views,
    Topicals, Real Photos
Edward Roth
P.O. Box 4252
Parkersburg, WV 26104
304-679-5609
Postcards, Covers, Postal Stationery
    (Used)

WISCONSIN

Roger L. Haag
Haag's Coins
Box 211
Sun Prairie, WI 53590
608-837-8042
Quality Real Photos, General Line,
    Views
Lois & Dale Heft
The Heft's of Madison
1305 Debra Lane
Madison, WI 53704
608-241-0851
Midwest States, Topics
Terry Kempf
205 Prairie St.
Lodi, WI 53555
608-592-5135
Madison WI, Dogs, Metamorphosis
Robert Koehler
4713 W. Nash
Milwaukee, WI 53216
414-442-4700

Milwaukee, Wisconsin, Baseball
Frank Lindemann
1313 Dakota St.
Watertown, WI 53094
414-261-0666
Joe Stransky
P.O. Box 1672
Madison, WI 53701
608-257-6240
U.S. Views, Postmarks, Foreign Views
Bernard White
White Postcard Co.
3304 Hwy. CC
Slinger, WI 53086
414-644-8478, 800-347-8478
Midwest Real Photos, Ships, World's
    Fair, Transportation, We Buy Cards

WYOMING

George & Evelyn Herman
Pack Rat Antiques
Box 2287
1008 8th St.
Cody, WY 82414
307-527-6560
American Indians

CANADA

John de la Vergne
676 Cooks Mills Rd.
North Bay, ONT P1B 8G3
705-497-3076
Canada, Real Photos
Larry Garfinkel
Garfinkel Publications
2784 W. 22nd Ave.

Vancouver, BC V6L 1M4
604-736-6912
Native Art, Historical Postcards,
    Cut-Out Postcards
Neil Hayne
P.O. Box 220, 147 Church St.
Bath, ONT K0H 1G0
613-352-7456
Topicals, Worldwide Views, Paper
    Canadiana
Donald Kaye
D. & L. Kaye Enterprises
P.O. Box 66660, Stoney Creek Postal
    Outlet
Stoney Creek, ONT L8G 5F6
416-957-7227
Canada, Postal History, Worldwide
Alison & Richard Moulton
216 Armit Ave.
Fort Frances, ONT P9A 2G9
807-274-6280
Subjects, Foreign Cards, Canada
Quality Stamps & Covers Inc.
P.O. Box 296
St. Albert, ALB T8N 1N3
403-460-2540
Transportation, USA Real Photo,
    Foreign
Michael J. Swiech
Silver Maple Stamps
P.O. Box 1899
Kingston, ONT K7L 5J7
613-545-0502
Ontario, Military

✳ 91

INDEX

This index to *Postcard Collector* provides a variety of listings that should prove valuable to researchers interested in learning more about the hobby of deltiology and specific cards, artists, etc. The index includes all issues from the magazine's beginning in November 1983 through February 1993. It will be updated yearly. Photocopies of specific references are available from *Postcard Collector* at a cost of 50 cents per page. Requests for photocopies should be directed to the Editor, *Postcard Collector*, P.O. Box 337, Iola, WI 54945.

11-89, 2-90, 9-90, 11-90, 2-91, 4-91, 8-91

PUBLISHER/DISTRIBUTOR INDEX

SERIES & SETS INDEX

✳ 99

✳ 101

SHOW CALENDAR

APRIL

Apr 2-3 NJ, Mt. Laurel. POCAX 93. 23rd Annual Exhibition of the South Jersey Post Card Club. Budget Motor Lodge, Exit 4 off NJ Tnpk. (adjacent to Trailways Bus Station). Fri. 10am-8pm, Sat. 10am-5pm, A: $1.50. 25 PC dealers. David Grubbs, 212 Kathy Dr., Yardley, PA 19067.

Apr 3 OH, New Philadelphia. 2nd Annual Tri-County Postcard Club Show. Riverfront Antique Mall, behind Best Western Inn (I-77 exit 81 to Rt. 39 east). 9am-4:30pm, A: free. 25-30 PC dealers. Ray Ferrel, 332 St. Clair Ave., Cadiz, OH 43907. PH: 614-942-3475.

Apr 3-4 CA, Santa Cruz. 7th California Central Coast Postcard & Paper Memorabilia Show (co-sponsored by San Jose, San Francisco & Santa Cruz Postcard Clubs). Holiday Inn, 611 Ocean. Sat. 10am-6pm, Sun. 10am-4pm, A: $1.00. Mike Rasmussen, P.O. Box 726, Marina, CA 93933. PH: 408-384-5460.

Apr 3-4 IL, Collinsville. 4th Metro-East Postcard Show. VFW Hall, 1234 Vandalia St. (Hwy 159, 15 min. from downtown St. Louis). Sat. 9am-6pm, Sun. 10am-4pm, A: free. 25 PC dealers. Holger (Danny) Danielsen, P.O. Box 1208, O'Fallon, IL 62269. PH: 1-800-548-5575.

Apr 4 NY, Levittown. Long Island Post Card Club Show. Israel Community Center, 3235 Hempstead Tpke. (Rt. 24, north side, west of Jerusalem Ave.). 10am-5pm, A: $2.00. Charles Huttunen, 9 Birmingham Dr., Northport, NY 11768. PH: 516-261-4031.

Apr 16-17 MD, Havre de Grace. The Chesapeake Postcard Fair. Policemen's Community Center, I-95 exit 89 (towards Havre de Grace, left on Graceview). Fri. 10am-7pm, Sat. 10am-5pm, A: $2.00. 40+ PC dealers. Mary L. Martin, 4899 Pulaski Hwy., Perryville, MD 21903. PH: 410-575-7768.

Apr 17 MI, Kalamazoo. SW Michigan Postcard Club Postcard Bourse. Kalamazoo County Fairgrounds, 2900 Lake St. 9am-4pm, A: free. 40 PC dealers. Sue Hodapp, 1415 Seminole St., Kalamazoo, MI 49006. PH: 616-344-2545.

Apr 17 PA, Pittsburgh. Three Rivers Postcard Club's Postcard & Paper Show. Mt. Lebanon United Methodist Church, 3319 W. Liberty Ave. 9am-4pm, A: $1.00. 25+ PC dealers. Richard Campbell, P.O. Box 25313, Pittsburgh, PA 15242. PH: 412-341-4522.

Apr 17-18 NC, Durham. Postcard Society Sale. Holiday Inn Durham-West, 3460 Hillsborough Rd. (just off I-85, southbound exit 174-B, northbound exit 173). Sat. 9am-6pm, Sun. 9am-3pm, A: free. 24 PC tables. John H. McClintock, Postcard Society, P.O. Box 1765, Manassas, VA 22110. PH: 703-368-2757.

Apr 18 IL, Rockford. Rock Valley Post Card Club Show. Forest Hills Lodge, 9900 Forest Hills Rd. (I-90 Riverside exit west to Forest Hills Rd. or Alpine Rd. north to Rt. 173). 10am-4pm, A: free. 15-20 PC dealers. George Gibson, 405 W. Hurlbut Ave., Belvidere, IL 61008. PH: 815-547-8558.

Apr 18 MA, East Watertown. Bay State Postcard Collectors Club Card-O-Rama 1993. Armenian Cultural & Educational Center, 47 Nichols Ave. 8:30am-3:30pm, A: free. 40 PC tables. Bill Crane, 898 Massachusetts Ave., Apt. 6, Arlington, MA 02174. PH: 617-646-3576.

Apr 18 OH, Columbus. Columbus Ohio Paper Fair. Vets Memorial Convention Center, 300 W. Broad St. 9am-4pm, A: $2.50. 15+ PC dealers. Sylvia Andromeda, 3280 Riverside Dr., Suite 18, Columbus, OH 43221. PH: 614-459-7469.

Apr 23-24 IL, Chicago. Greater Chicago Postcard & Ephemera Show. Hillside Holiday Inn, I-290 & Mannheim (15 min. south of O'Hare Airport). Fri. 10am-8pm, Sat. 10am-4pm. $3.00/day, $5.00/show. 40-45 PC dealers. Susan Brown Nicholson, P.O. Box 595, Lisle, IL 60532. PH: 708-964-5240.

Apr 24 OR, Gresham. Webfooters Postcard Club Show & Sale. National Guard Armory, 500 N.E. Division (on 5 north, take exit 205 east, then exit Division St. east; on 5 south, take exit 30, 84 east, then exit 205 south to exit Division St. east; on 30, 84 west, take exit 13 to 181st south to exit Division St. east). 10am-5pm, A: free. 25 PC dealers. Doris Brockell, 5014 N.E. 26th, Portland, OR 07211 6315. PH: 503-282-2130. Steve Kenney, 31841 E. Crown Point Hwy., Troutdale, OR 97060. PH: 503-695-5151.

Apr 24-25 CA, San Diego. Greater San Diego Postcard & Paper Collectibles Show. Al Bahr Temple, 5440 Kearny Mesa at the 163 Frwy. and Clairemont Mesa. Sat. 10am-6pm, Sun. 10am-4pm. Nick Farago, P.O. Box 217, Temple City, CA 91780. PH: 818-287-6066.

Apr 25 CT, Meriden. 12th Annual Connecticut Postcard Club Bourse. Ramada Inn, 275 Research Pkwy. (East Main St. exits off I-91 or Rte. 15). 8:30-10am members only, 10am-5pm general public, A: $2.00, $1.50/ad or flyer. 45 PC dealers. Peter Maronn, 180 Goodwin St., Bristol, CT 06010. PH: 203-589-6984.

Apr 25 NY, Stamford. 15th Annual Post Card Show. V.F.W. Post, Rt. 10 (3/4 mile beyond Red Carpet Motor Inn). 9am-5pm. 25 PC tables. Carlton Bloodgood, Bogota, NJ 07603.

Apr 30-May 2 NY, New York. 16th International Post Card Bourse. Days Inn, 440 W. 57th St. Fri. 11am-7pm, Sat. 10am-7pm, Sun. 11am-5pm, A: $3.00. 65+ PC dealers. Leah Schnall, 67-00 192 St., Flushing NY 11365. PH: 718-454-0582.

MAY

May 1 CA, Montecito. Santa Barbara Postcard & Paper Collectibles Show. Mira Mar Hotel, 1555 S. Jameson Ln. Saturday only 10am-6pm. Nick Farago, P.O. Box 217, Temple City, CA 91780. PH: 818-287-6066.

May 1 OH, Columbus. Heart of Ohio Post Card Club Spring Show. Quality Inn, E. Broad & Hamilton Rd. 10am,-4pm, A: $1.50. Ron Hilbert, P.O. Box 67, Unionville Center, OH 43077. PH: 614-873-4552.

May 1-2 IN, Indianapolis. 18th Annual Indianapolis Post Card Club Show. Indiana State Fairgrounds, SW Pavilion, 1202 E. 38th St. Sat. 9am-6pm, Sun 10am-4pm, A: $2.00. 30+ PC dealers. John McDonough, 5881 Downing Dr., Indianapolis, IN 46208-1635. PH: 317-290-9276.

May 7-8 OH, Olmsted Falls. Western Reserve Postcard Society Show. Lenau Park, 7370 Columbia Rd. (Rt. 252 south of I-480). Fri. 11am-7pm, Sat. 10am-4pm, A: $1.00. 36 PC dealers. Paul Knapp, 25028 Rainbow Dr., Olmsted Falls, OH 44138. PH: 216-234-4441.

May 8 MD, Towson. Towson Postcard & Paper Show. Quality Inn, 1015 York Rd. (I-695 to exit 26A, behind Howard Johnson's). 10am-4pm, A: free. 11+ PC dealers. Dee Delcher, Maryland Postcard Society, 413 E. Lake Ave., Baltimore, MD 21212. PH: 410-433-1532.

May 8 WV, Clarksburg. West Virginia Postcard & Paper Show. Holiday Inn-Bridgeport, I-79 & US 50. 9am-5pm, A: free. 7+ PC dealers. Edward Roth, WV Postal History Society, P.O. Box 4252, Parkersburg, WV 26104. PH: 304-679-5609.

May 8-9 TN, Knoxville. Tennessee Postcard Association Show. Quality Inn West, I-40/75 & West Hills Exit. Sat. 9am-6pm, Sun. 10am-5pm, A: free. 20 PC dealers. Paul E. Garland, 1919 Rosemont Circle, Louisville, TN 37777. PH: 615-970-3271.

May 14-15 PA, York. Ye Old Valley Post Card Show. York Mall, 2801 E. Market St. on Rt. 462 (exit 8 off I-83). 10am-9pm, A: free. Jerry Kotek, 424 Corbin Rd., York, PA 17403. PH: 717-843-3479.

May 16 IA, Cedar Rapids. Cedar Rapids Postcard Show. Sheraton Inn, 525 33rd Ave. SW. 9am-6pm, A: free. 25 PC dealers. Vivian Rinaberger, 4548 Fairlane Dr. NE, Cedar Rapids, IA 52402. PH: 319-393-6743.

May 16 ME, Portland. Pinetree Postcard Club's Annual Spring Show. Italian Heritage Center, off Congress St. behind Shaw's Westgate. 9am-4pm, A: $1.00. 35 PC dealers. John Vierra, P.O. Box 6783, Portland, ME 04101. PH: 207-657-4399.

May 22 NY, Slate Hill. 14th Annual Half Moon Postcard Club, Inc., Show & Sale. Minisink Valley High School, Route 6 (Orange County, 10 min. west of Middletown, NY). 9am-5pm, A: $1.00. 40 PC dealers. Dee Dee Backus, 636 Greenville Tnpk., Port Jervis, NY 12771. PH: 914-856-3461.

May 23 WI, Milwaukee. Milwaukee Postcard Collectors Club Show. Gonzaga Hall, 1441 S. 92nd St. 10am-5pm, A: $1.00. 25 PC dealers. Frank Greiczek, 3041 N. Humboldt, Milwaukee, WI 53212. PH: 414-264-0225.

May 28-29 MD, Hagerstown. Postcard Society Sale. Howard Johnson Hotel, 107 Underpass Way (exit #5 off I-81 to traffic light, then 2 left turns). Fri. 9am-6pm, Sat. 9am-3pm, A: free. 40 PC tables. John H. McClintock, Postcard Society, P.O. Box 1765, Manassas, VA 22110. PH: 703-368-2757.

May 29-30 KS, Merriam. 11th Annual Heart of America Postcard Collectors Show. Merriam Community Center, 5701 Merriam Dr. (Johnson Dr. exit off I-35, right to traffic light, right three blocks). Sat. 9am-6pm, Sun. 9am-4pm. Don Harmon 12806 W. 71st St., Shawnee, KS 66216. PH: 913-268-6149.

JUNE

Jun 4-5 IL, LaGrange/Countryside. Windy City Postcard Show. International Union of Operating Engineers Hall, 6200 Joliet Rd. (1/2 block west of LaGrange Rd.). Fri. 10am-8pm, Sat. 10am-4pm, A: $2.00. 40 PC dealers. Gene Palys, WCPC, P.O. Box 818, LaGrange, IL 60525.

Jun 4-6 CA, Pasadena. Greater LA Postcard & Paper Collectibles Show. Elks Hall, 400 W. Colorado Blvd. Fri. early bird 11am-1pm, public 1-8pm, Sat. 10am-6pm, Sun. 10am-4pm. Nick Farago, P.O. Box 217, Temple City, CA 91780. PH: 818-287-6066.

Jun 6 NY, Oswego. Oswego County Postcard Club Show. Scriba Fire Hall, 2 miles east of Oswego on Rte. 10. 10am-5pm, A: $1.00. 23 PC dealers. Lillian M. McCloskey, 7 W. 8th St., Oswego, NY. PH: 315-343-1049.

Jun 6 OH, Cincinnati. Don Skillman's 9th Annual June Postcard Show. Ramada Hotel, 5901 Pfeiffer Rd. & I-71 (exit 15). 9am-5pm, A: $2.00. 22 PC dealers. Don Skillman, 6646 Shiloh Rd., Goshen, OH 45122. PH: 513-625-9518.

Jun 6 PA, Shamokin Dam. 8th Annual Susquehanna Valley Post Card Club Show. Days Inn, Rts. 11 & 15 (across bridge from Sunbury). 9am-4pm, A: $1.00. Roy H. Shoop, 108 Maple Ln., Watsontown, PA 17777-1308.

Jun 13 BC, Vancouver. Vancouver Postcard Club Show. Hastings Community Center, 3096 E. Hastings St. 9am-4pm, A: early bird $5.00, general $1.00. 25 PC dealers. Lance Arnett, 2260 King Albert Ave., Coquitlam, BC, Canada V3J 1Z5.

Jun 19 OH, Ashland. Johnny Appleseed Postcard Club Show. Ashland High School, corner Katherine Ave. & King Rd. 8am-4:30pm, A: $1.00. 30 PC dealers. John Wagenhals, P.O. Box 801, Ashland, OH 44805. PH: 419-281-1997.

Jun 26-27 WA, Kent. Greater Seattle Postcard & Paper Collectibles Show. Kent Commons, 525 4th Ave. North. Sat. 10am-6pm, Sun. 10am-4pm. Nick Farago, P.O. Box 217, Temple City, CA 91780. PH: 818-287-6066.

JULY

Jul 9-10 PA, York. 3rd Annual York Post Card Club Show. Aldergate Church, Tyler Run Rd. (I-83 exit 6 north, 1st light on Queen St.). Fri. 10am-6pm, Sat. 9am-5pm, A: $1.50. Jerry Kotek, 424 Corbin Rd., York, PA 17403. PH: 717-843-3479.

Jul 9-11 CA, San Francisco. Greater San Francisco Bay Area Postcard & Paper Collectibles Show. Holiday Inn, 1221 Chess Dr. (Foster City Blvd. exit off Hwy. 92). Fri. 10am-8pm, Sat. 10am-6pm, Sun. 10am-4pm. Nick Farago, P.O. Box 217, Temple City, CA 91780. PH: 818-287-6066.

Jul 16-18 CO, Denver. Rocky Mountain States Postcard Show. Super 8 Hotel, 2601 Zuni St. (exit 212B off I-25 at Speer Blvd.). Fri. 6-9:30pm earlybird, Sat. 9am-5pm, Sun. 10am-4pm, A: $1.00, early bird $5.00.

25-30 PC dealers. George Van Trump, P.O. Box 260170, Lakewood, CO 80226-0170. PH: 303-985-3508. Erwin Engert. PH: 303-986-8516.

Jul 24-25 MO, Hannibal. 2nd Annual Postcard Show of the Mark Twain Postcard Club of the Tri-State Area. Holiday Inn, Hwy. 61 S. Sat. 9am-5pm, Sun. 9am-4pm, A: free. 30+ PC dealers. Sally Polc, 24 Brown Estates, Hannibal, MO 63401. PH: 314-248-1216.

Jul 24-25 VA, Harrisonburg. Shenandoah Valley Postcard Show. Ramada Inn (formerly Holiday Inn), I-81 exit 243 at Rt. 11. Sat. 10am-6pm, Sun. 11am-4pm, A: $1.50. 14 PC dealers. Jeff Bradfield, 745 Hillview Dr., Dayton, VA 22821. PH: 703-879-9961.

Jul 31-Aug 1 TX, Ft. Worth. Cowtown Postcard Club Annual Show. Holiday Inn North, I-35 at Meacham Blvd. Sat. 10am-6pm, Sun. 10am-4pm, A: $1.00 Sat. only. 20-22 PC dealers. Ruth Scott, 1615 Bluebonnet Dr., Fort Worth, TX 76111. PH: 817-834-0103.

AUGUST

Aug 13-14 IL, Chicago. Greater Chicago Postcard & Ephemera Show. Hillside Holiday Inn, I-290 & Mannheim (15 min. south of O'Hare Airport). Fri. 10am-8pm, Sat. 10am-4pm. $3.00/day, $5.00/show. 40-45 PC dealers. Susan Brown Nicholson, P.O. Box 595, Lisle, IL 60532. PH: 708-964-5240.

Aug 14 CA, Montecito. Santa Barbara Postcard & Paper Collectibles Show. Mira Mar Hotel, 1555 S. Jameson Ln. Saturday only 10am-6pm. Nick Farago, P.O. Box 217, Temple City, CA 91780. PH: 818-287-6066.

Aug 14 NJ, Woodbridge. 3rd Annual Central Jersey Deltiological Society Post Card Event. Budget Motor Lodge, 350 Rt. 9 North. 10am-4:30pm, A: $1.00. 30 PC dealers. Norm Bobel, 518 Front St., Dunellen, NJ 08812-1010 (SASE). PH: 908-968-4249.

Aug 21 PA, Lancaster. Lancaster Co. Postcard Club Expo. Farm & Home Center, 1383 Arcadia Rd. (off Rt. 72 behind Jones Pontiac). 9am-6pm, A: $1.00/ad. 25 PC dealers. Jose Rodriguez, P.O. Box 903, Cheshire, CT 06410. Jim Ward, P.O. Box 300, Lititz, PA 17543.

Aug 28-29 KY, Louisville. Annual Louisville Postcard Show. Hurstbourne Hotel, Bluegrass Pkwy. (just off I-64). Sat. 9am-6pm, Sun. 9am-4pm, A: $2.00. 27 PC dealers. Don Skillman, 6646 Shiloh Rd., Goshen, OH 45122. PH: 513-625-9518.

Aug 29 MT, Helena. Fall 1993 Montana Postcard & Paper Show. Colonial Inn. 10am-5pm, A: $1.00. 5-8 PC dealers. Tom Mulvaney, Box 814, East Helena, MT 59635. PH: 406-227-8790.

SEPTEMBER

Sep 11 MD, Towson. Towson Postcard & Paper Show. Quality Inn, 1015 York Rd. (I-695 to exit 26A, behind Howard Johnson's). 10am-4pm, A: free. 11+ PC dealers. Dee Delcher, Maryland Postcard Society, 413 E. Lake Ave., Baltimore, MD 21212. PH: 410-433-1532.

Sep 11 OR, Oak Grove. Willamette Valley Post Card Club Show & Sale. Oak Grove Community Club, 14496 SE Cedar St. (99E exit north off I-205 for 5 mi., left on Courtney). 10am-4pm, A: free. 10-15 PC dealers. Nancy Lewis, 530 Middlecrest Rd., Lake Oswego, OR 97034.

Sep 11-12 MN, St. Paul. Twin City Postcard Club Fall Show. The Kelly Inn, I-94 at Marion St. exit. Sat. 10am-6pm, Sun. 9am-3pm, A: $1.50. 15 PC dealers. W.R. Everett, 111 Marquette, #1202, Minneapolis, MN 55401-2029. PH: 612-333-2219.

Sep 12 OH, Columbus. Columbus Ohio Paper Fair. Vets Memorial Convention Center, 300 W. Broad St. 9am-4pm, A: $2.50. 15+ PC dealers. Sylvia Andromeda, 3280 Riverside Dr., Suite 18, Columbus, OH 43221. PH: 614-459-7469.

Sep 17-18 NJ, Mt. Laurel. Postcard Society Sale. Budget Motor Lodge, Route #73 & Fellowship Rd. Fri. 9am-6pm, Sat. 9am-3pm, A: free. 40+ PC tables. John H. McClintock, Postcard Society, P.O. Box 1765, Manassas, VA 22110. PH: 703-368-2757.

Sep 17-18 OH, Columbus. 18th Annual Heart of Ohio Post Card Show. Aladdin Temple, 3850 Stelzer Rd. (I-270 Morse Rd. exit). Fri. 9am-6pm, Sat. 9am-4pm, A: $1.50/two days. 40 PC dealers. Betty Sidle, 444 Heather Lane, Powell, OH 43065. PH: 614-548-5265.

Sep 18 NY, Schenectady. Upstate NY Postcard Club Show. Shaughnessy Hall, 1 S. Church St. (NYS Thrwy. west exit 25, east exit 26 to Washington Ave. exit #4, turn right one block). 9am-5pm, A: $1.00. 28

PC dealers. Jim Davis, 5 Cutter Dr., Johnstown, NY 12095. PH: 518-762-8659.

Sep 19 CT, Litchfield. 16th Litchfield Postcard Show. Litchfield Fire House, 258 West St., Rte. 202. 9:30am-4:30pm, A: $1.00, free to CT Postcard Club members. 18 PC dealers. Peter Maronn, CT Postcard Club, 180 Goodwin St. Bristol, CT 06010. PH: 203-589-6984.

Sep 24-26 CA, Pasadena. Greater LA Postcard & Paper Collectibles Show. Elks Hall, 400 W. Colorado Blvd. Fri. early bird 11am-1pm, public 1-8pm, Sat. 10am-6pm, Sun. 10am-4pm. Nick Farago, P.O. Box 217, Temple City, CA 91780. PH: 818-287-6066.

Sep 25 IA, Clive (Des Moines). Hawkeye Postcard Club of Des Moines Show. Travelodge Des Moines-West, 11001 University Ave. 9am-5pm, A: free. 16 PC dealers. A. Aller. PH: 515-279-5418.

Sep 25 MA, Dennis (Cape Cod). 8th Annual Postcard Show & Sale. Dennis Senior Citizens Center, Rte. 134 & Setucket Rd. (exit 9 off Mid-Cape Hwy./Rte. 6, north on Rte. 134 two miles). 9:30am-4:30pm, A: $1.00. 30 PC dealers. Helen Angell, Short Neck Rd., So. Dennis, MA 02660. PH: 508-398-1793.

Sep 25 PA, Pittsburgh. Three Rivers Postcard Club's Postcard & Paper Show. Mt. Lebanon United Methodist Church, 3319 W. Liberty Ave. 9am-4pm, A: $1.00. 25+ PC dealers. Richard Campbell, P.O. Box 25313, Pittsburgh, PA 15242. PH: 412-341-4522.

Sep 25-26 TN, Knoxville. Tennessee Postcard Association Show. Quality Inn West, I-40/75 & West Hills Exit. Sat. 9am-6pm, Sun. 10am-5pm, A: free. 20 PC dealers. Paul E. Garland, 1919 Rosemont Circle, Louisville, TN 37777. PH: 615-970-3271.

Sep 26 ONT, Burlington. The Golden Horseshoe Post Card Club Show & Sale. Central Arena Auditorium, 519 Drury Lane. 10am-5pm, A: free. 25 PC dealers. Paul McWhinnie, P.O. Box 66660, Stoney Creek, Ontario, Canada L8G 5E6.

OCTOBER

Oct 3 PA, Wind Gap. Lehigh Valley Post Card Club Show. Plainfield Township Fire Co., Sullivan Trail (1 mi. south of Wind Gap). 9am-4pm, A: $1.00. 40-45 PC dealers. Gene Mickel, 201 Prospect St., Phillipsburg, NJ 08865. PH: 908-859-4242 after 5pm.

Oct 9-10 NJ, Parsippany. 34th Annual Garden State Post Card Collectors Club Post Card Show. P.A.L. Center, 33 Baldwin Rd. (off Rt. 46 at Burger King). Sat. 10am-7pm, Sun. 10am-5pm, A: $1.00. 40+ PC dealers. Dolores Kirchgessner, 421 Washington St., Hoboken, NJ 07030. PH: 201-659-1922.

Oct 9-10 OR, Portland. Greater Portland Postcard & Paper Collectibles Show. Portland Scottish Rite Temple, 709 S.W. 15th (at Morrison St.). Sat. 10am-6pm, Sun. 10am-4pm. Nick Farago, P.O. Box 217, Temple City, CA 91780. PH: 818-287-6066.

Oct 10 IA, Cedar Rapids. Cedar Rapids Postcard Show. Sheraton Inn, 525 33rd Ave. SW. 9am-6pm, A: free. 25 PC dealers. Vivian Rinaberger, 4548 Fairlane Dr. NE, Cedar Rapids, IA 52402. PH: 319-393-6743.

Oct 10 IN, Indianapolis. Crossroads of America Postcard Show. Indiana State Fairgrounds, Southwest Pavilion (Senior Citizens Bldg.). 9am-5pm, A: $2.00. George Mitchell, 2145 N. Talbott Ave., Indianapolis, IN 46202. PH: 317-924-0712.

Oct 16-17 KS, Wichita. 16th Wichita International. All Saints' Gym, 3313 Grand (NE of Hillside & Harry Sts.). Sat. 9am-6pm, Sun. 10am-4pm, A: free. 35-40 PC dealers. John Pittman, 3900 N. St. Clair, Wichita, KS 67204. PH: 316-838-3038.

Oct 23 MI, Kalamazoo. SW Michigan Postcard Club Postcard Bourse. Kalamazoo County Fairgrounds, 2900 Lake St. 9am-4pm, A: free. 40 PC dealers. Sue Hodapp, 1415 Seminole St., Kalamazoo, MI 49006. PH: 616-344-2545.

Oct 24 NY, Newark. 18th Annual Post Card Show & Sale of the Western New York Post Card Club. Newark Quality Motel, 125 N. Main St. (Rt. 88, north of Barge Canal off Rt. 31). 9am-4pm, A: $2.00. Edward J. Beiderbecke, P.O. Box 155, Williamson, NY 14589. PH: 315-589-2287.

Oct 24 WI, Milwaukee. Milwaukee Postcard Collectors Club Show. Gonzaga Hall, 1441 S. 92nd St. 10am-5pm, A: $1.00. 25 PC dealers. Frank Greiczek, 3041 N. Humboldt, Milwaukee, WI 53212. PH: 414-264-0225.

NOVEMBER

Nov 5-7 NY, New York. 47th Annual Metro Postcard Club Bourse. Days Inn, 440 W. 57th St. Fri. 11am-

7pm, Sat. 10am-7pm, Sun. 11am-5pm, A: $3.00. 65+ PC dealers. Leah Schnall, 67-00 192 St., Flushing NY 11365. PH: 718-454-0582.

Nov 13-14 IL, Bloomington. CORNPEX '93. Scottish Rite Temple, near intersection of northbound U.S. Rte. 51 & eastbound IL Rte. 9. Sat. 10am-6pm, Sun. 10am-4pm, A: free. 15 PC dealers. Janice Jenkins, Corn Belt Philatelic Society, Box 625, Bloomington, IL 61702-0625. PH: 309-663-2761.

Nov 13-14 VA, Ashland. Postcard Society Sale. Best Western Motel, off I-95 Atlee-Elmont exit (about 10 miles north of Richmond). Sat. 9am-6pm, Sun. 9am-3pm, A: $1.00. 33 PC tables. John H. McClintock, Postcard Society, P.O. Box 1765, Manassas, VA 22110. PH: 703-368-2757.

Nov 19-20 IL, Chicago. Greater Chicago Postcard & Ephemera Show. Hillside Holiday Inn, I-290 & Mannheim (15 min. south of O'Hare Airport). Fri. 10am-8pm, Sat. 10am-4pm. $3.00/day, $5.00/show. 40-45 PC dealers. Susan Brown Nicholson, P.O. Box 595, Lisle, IL 60532. PH: 708-964-5240.

Nov 19-20 PA, York. York International Postcard Fair, York Fairgrounds, Rt. 83 to 30 west to 74 south. Fri. 9am-7pm, Sat. 9am-5pm, A: $2.00. 50+ PC dealers. Mary L. Martin, 4899 Pulaski Hwy., Perryville, MD 21903.

Nov 21 CA, Arcadia. San Gabriel Valley Postcard & Paper Collectibles Show. Masonic Hall, 50 W. Duarte Rd. Sunday only 10am-6pm. Nick Farago, P.O. Box 217, Temple City, CA 91780. PH: 818-287-6066.

DECEMBER

Dec 4-5 CA, San Diego. Greater San Diego Postcard & Paper Collectibles Show. Al Bahr Temple, 5440 Kearny Mesa at the 163 Frwy. and Clairemont Mesa. Sat. 10am-6pm, Sun. 10am-4pm. Nick Farago, P.O. Box 217, Temple City, CA 91780. PH: 818-287-6066.

Dec 18 MD, Towson. Towson Postcard & Paper Show. Quality Inn, 1015 York Rd. (I-695 to exit 26A, behind Howard Johnson's). 10am-4pm, A: free. 11+ PC dealers. Dee Delcher, Maryland Postcard Society, 413 E. Lake Ave., Baltimore, MD 21212. PH: 410-433-1532.

1994
JANUARY

Jan 29 MD, Elkton. Paper Americana Show. Singerly Fire Hall, Rts. 213 & 279 (Elkton/Newark, DE, exit off I-95). 10am-4pm, A: $1.50. 12+ PC dealers. Jeri Ayers, 3868 Telegraph Rd., Elkton, MD 21921. PH: 410-398-7735.

APRIL

Apr 2 OH, New Philadelphia. 3rd Annual Tri-County Postcard Club Show. Riverfront Antique Mall, behind Best Western Inn (I-77 exit 81 to Rt. 39 east). 9am-4:30pm, A: free. 25-30 PC dealers. Ray Ferrel, 332 St. Clair Ave., Cadiz, OH 43907. PH: 614-942-3475.

Apr 9-10 IL, Collinsville. 5th Metro-East Postcard Show. VFW Hall, 1234 Vandalia St. (Hwy. 159, 15 min. from downtown St. Louis), Sat. 9am-6pm, Sun. 10am-4pm, A: free. 20-25 PC dealers. Holger (Danny) Danielsen, P.O. Box 1208, O'Fallon, IL 62269. PH: 1-800-548-5575.

Apr 17 IL, Rockford. Rock Valley Post Card Club Show. Location to be announced. 10am-4pm, A: free. 15 PC dealers. Robert Swanson, 924 17th St., Rockford, IL 61104. PH: 815-398-5384.

MAY

May 20-22 NY, New York. 17th International Post Card Bourse. Days Inn, 440 W. 57th St. Fri. 11am-7pm, Sat. 10am-7pm, Sun. 11am-5pm, A: $3.00. 65+ PC dealers. Leah Schnall, 67-00 192 St., Flushing NY 11365. PH: 718-454-0582.

AUGUST

Aug 20 NJ, Woodbridge. 4th Annual Post Card Event. Budget Motor Lodge, 350 Rte. 9 North (send #10 SASE for directions). 10am-4:30pm, A: $1.00. 27 PC dealers. Norman Bobel, 518 Front St., Dunellen, NJ 08812-1010. PH: 908-968-4249.

NOVEMBER

Nov 11-13 NY, New York. 48th Annual Metro Postcard Club Bourse. Days Inn, 440 W. 57th St. Fri. 11am-7pm, Sat. 10am-7pm, Sun. 11am-5pm, A: $3.00. 65+ PC dealers. Leah Schnall, 67-00 192 St., Flushing NY 11365. PH: 718-454-0582.

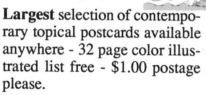

ADVERTISING INDEX